# Praise for *Re*

"Anderson strikes gold with his take on how to live our golden years. When many are taking their foot off the gas, he suggests a more satisfying and intentional path. He shares fresh insights on leveraging work experience, finding true purpose, and contributing value in the later years of life. You'll learn ways to repurpose your wisdom and experience to leave a lasting legacy in your family, your community, and the world. Brimming with possibility, Replace Retirement is a call to action, a celebration, and a how-to manual for the second half—the best half—of life."

—CHIP CONLEY, entrepreneur, author of
*Wisdom at Work: The Making of a Modern Elder*

"Writer Albert Flynn DeSilver argues that, 'time is not something that you have or don't have, time is something you create.' With this great new book, John Anderson shows us how to create more time—time to live our dreams, time to make a difference, time to make our world a better and more interesting place. If you're heading towards—or are at—midlife and feeling like time is running out, think again. And then make time to read this mind-opening book!"

—ARI WEINZWEIG, noted author and founding
partner of Zingerman's Community of Businesses

"Jaw-dropping, inspiring, incredibly well researched. I've read it over and over! If you're in your 50s or 60s and thinking about retiring, you're crazy—particularly in light of John's compelling argument that these are the absolute best years of your life. I could not agree more and nobody has done a more compelling job to inspire Baby Boomers to seize life! I personally recommend this book to everyone, even in their 20s or 30s, to know what they can look forward to. Life keeps getting better and better, particularly if you adopt John's mindset—the second half of your life will be spectacular!"

—PAUL AKERS, founder and CEO of FastCap and author of *2 Second Lean*

"Wow! Captivating reading. John uses himself as an example and cites quotations from Socrates to Warren Buffett to prove his theory that we should never 'retire.' I am in full agreement with John setting his life expectancy at 103. If you are 45 years of age or older, this book is a must-read. Order your copy of this book right now and set the plan in motion to guarantee you live a long, happy, and productive life."

—PETER H. THOMAS, noted author, chairman emeritus EO, founder and CEO Thomas Franchise Solutions, LTD

"John Anderson has written the best practical user's guide yet for those who have decided that the whole concept and structure of 'retirement' is not for them. Count me in as a long-time member of this 'keep growing until you drop' club. In a decade or so we'll see that the very idea of formal mandatory retirement is as obsolete for most people as mindless shift work in industrial-age factories."

—DAN SULLIVAN, founder of The Strategic Coach, Inc.

"John cut his teeth on helping execs achieve their maximum potential. Now he's on a bold mission to disrupt the retirement paradigm by helping Baby Boomers and others ignite their destiny! Articulating a personal strategy that's both visionary and achievable can seem over-whelming. But with Anderson's unique Legacy Map, you'll be focused and equipped to tackle the second half of life—the best half—with a powerful, exponential purpose. This book is your guide to living intentionally and creating a legacy every day."

—JOSH LINKNER, author of *Disciplined Dreaming*, *The Road to Reinvention*, and *Hacking Innovation*

"You have the gift and I am thankful our team gets to be around it. You are in your prime 'wisdom spot' right now and I am looking forward to many more years of being around your gift."

—MICHAEL SCHMIDT, president, Coldwell Banker Schmidt Family of Companies

ISBN    978-1-5445-0121-5    Paperback
          978-1-5445-0122-2    Ebook
          978-1-5445-0123-9    Audiobook

LIONCREST
PUBLISHING

# REPLACE
## RETIREMENT

### Living Your Legacy in
### the Exponential Age

## John D. Anderson

Foreword by McKeel Hagerty
Edited by Karl Nilsson

"Action without vision is only passing the time. Vision without action is merely daydreaming. But vision with action can change the world."

—NELSON MANDELA

# CONTENTS

# ACKNOWLEDGMENTS

I wish to thank my wife, Molly, for being not only my beloved life partner, but also an amazing editorial contributor to Karl Nilsson and myself, and for driving clarity for the entire Replace Retirement team. Karl's input and writing over the many months took my ideas from concept to reality and added a more personal touch to the narrative.

Along the way, numerous clients and peers contributed greatly to the Legacy Map evolution by using and promoting the tool. In particular, Jim Agley's great insight and adaptation allowed me to modify the original Success Map to the current Legacy Map. Jim pushed me into thinking long term and about what matters most versus the insatiable quest for material and business success.

I'm grateful to the Young Presidents' Organization (YPO) Grand Rapids chapter, specifically to members of the White Out Forum and McKeel Hagerty. My Detroit Entrepreneurs' Organization (EO) Catalyst Forum table (we celebrated our 20th anniversary) has been an ongoing source of inspiration for pursuing my life purpose: to inspire and challenge leaders to achieve their greatest personal potential.

Verne Harnish, founder of EO and my personal "Obi-Wan Kenobi," has immeasurably influenced my lifelong commitment to learning and growth. From the beginning, Verne graciously provided my gateway to people and opportunities. Friends and authors like

Peter Thomas, Peter Diamandis, Patrick Lencioni, Paul Akers, Dan Sullivan, Ari Weinzweig, and others have mentored me formally and informally to think exponentially about my life and impact.

My children, John and Katie, and their mother, Cindy, have all enriched my life and legacy by imparting their own identity and unique qualities. Their humility, wisdom, and generosity inspire me. Thanks to Michael Cauley for believing in me 100 percent of the time and being my wingman. Finally, thanks to the Farbman Group, not only for being a 15-year client, but also for trusting me during the times I was struggling to believe in myself.

# FOREWORD

## By McKeel Hagerty

The day I met John Anderson, he extended my life by 12 years.

That's how powerful the ideas are in this book. They are not just life-extending, they are life-changing.

Let me take you back to the day in 2011 when I first met John. I am 39-years-old and John is consulting with my small YPO (Young Presidents' Organization) forum group in Grand Rapids, Michigan. Several members already know him—he's been their business coach for years. Yet he is new to the rest of us and we are a demanding lot. But based on what our colleagues have told us about him, we are willing to hear what he has to say.

We spend the first half of the session talking about habit formation and the concepts in the book *The Compound Effect* by Darren Hardy. The ideas in the book are powerful and resonate with many of us. Real change, Hardy says, takes longer—sometimes years longer—than we think, whether it's a fitness plan or a business concept. Many of us quit long before we see the fruits of our efforts, and the main culprit seems to be our unwillingness to commit sufficient time to the change process and to our inability to track concrete results.

We also talk extensively about the tools needed to create and measure successful habits and change in our lives. In addition to creating realistic timeframes, both Hardy and John recommend diligent tracking. "What gets measured, gets done"—so the standard coaching line goes. Several of us commit right then and there to tracking our habit-forming results and creating personal Key Performance Indicators (KPIs). We also create accountability pairs that require weekly check-ins about our progress or lack thereof.

We don't know it at the time but many in the forum group—including me—will come to consider the months and years following the adoption of these habits as the most life-changing period of our adult lives. Almost every day since, I have tracked on a spreadsheet the major data points I have needed to create and sustain excellence in my life. Whenever people ask how I get so much done, I often point to my tracking of habits and personal KPIs as my cornerstone.

If that was all I learned that day, I would be forever grateful to John. But the life-changing insights were only beginning. During the second half of our time together, John focuses on his Legacy Map, a worksheet he is developing to help people focus on a full-life view of success. And to prove his point, he asks for a volunteer from our group to be the guinea pig. Naturally, I raise my hand.

John asks me in front of the group to name the age I will be when I die. This exercise begins with a visioning of the final year of my life. Caught quickly in the mental bind of wanting a long life but not wanting to be greedy for years, I choose 88. He then takes me through a process where I describe in detail what my life looks like at the beginning of my 88th year. I describe where I will live, what my houses look like, what my marriage and relationships with my children and grandchildren will be like. I talk about my health and vitality regimen—jokingly adjusted for my 88-year-old body. I talk about my financial security, how I will spend my time, how happy and fulfilled I am. By the end of it, I am one fricking happy, healthy, and successful 88-year-old!

John smiles as he listens and takes careful notes. He reads highlights of my end-of-life vision back to me and the group and then looks me in the eye and asks, "McKeel, if you are such a happy, healthy, and successful guy at 88, why are you going to die so young?" We all laugh. I squirm a bit. And then I have an epiphany unlike any I have ever experienced. It is like someone revealing to me some sort of chronological Holy Grail, or more properly, a fountain of youth. I blurt out, "OK, then, 100. I will die at 100." John laughs again and says: "I just added 12 years to your life!"

And I have not given those 12 years back since.

John and I have met privately countless times since the forum meeting to discuss transformative ideas and concepts. His work with people like me is now focused largely on what we call the second half of life. This term was introduced to both of us by Richard Rohr in his book, *Falling Upward*. Rohr challenges the typical understanding of the cycle of life that somewhere in the middle of it we start a decline toward death. Probably based mostly on a realization that our bodies are no longer youthful in the later years of our life, we simply apply the notion of decline to every dimension. Even for the most fortunate of people, the latter "half" of life will be a gigantic compromise. We won't like it, we won't want to be there, and we will rail against it with mostly superficial cures. Rohr challenges these notions and offers a different view. Maybe, he says, we won't miss the things we think we'll miss in the second half of life. Instead, maybe we'll find alternatives of greater meaning and substance that make the second half of life better than the first.

This is John Anderson's new territory in *Replace Retirement.*

We are entering a new age of humanity, an exponential age where change and progress are accelerating faster than human minds can grasp. Everywhere we look, incredible abundance and opportunity are emerging and life, by almost any measure, is progressing. Almost without fail, people across the globe—beginning with this generation—will see exponential improvements in health, wealth, and quality of life, and for those with an abundant view of life, old barriers and obstacles will fall by the wayside, ushering in an era of possibility.

This era will dare the courageous to recalibrate and ask themselves what really matters: *What makes a good life? How will we measure it? How will we (or should we) think about the second half?* Even more provocatively: *What are the things we might be able to do better in the latter half of our life?* I won't steal John's thunder but will let you discover for yourself these new opportunities for insight and substance.

In perhaps the most famous soliloquy in dramatic history—yes, the "to be, or not to be" speech—Shakespeare's Hamlet describes life after death as the "undiscovered country," a place unknown and worthy of fear. Perhaps the new afterlife is right in front of us, and it's right here on earth. Perhaps it is the new years of perspective and wisdom we will experience as a result of the exponential age. Perhaps the new priority for us is not immortality but vitality and wisdom in our second half of life. Perhaps there are vast landscapes of meaning and value to be found in the bounty of our longer lives. It's exciting to think about.

Let us go boldly into this new territory. Let this book be our guide.

# INTRODUCTION

**By Verne Harnish**

In 1963, Bob Dylan sang "the times, they are a-changin'."

That's especially true in the Exponential Age that's sweeping the globe.

We live in a time of drastic, nonlinear change. A time when yesterday's answers don't work anymore. And yesterday's retirement model is obsolete.

My longtime friend, John Anderson, is challenging people over 50 to apply their invaluable life skills to a higher calling—during what used to be called the "retirement years." John is showing Baby Boomers and others how to leverage their unique contribution to pursue new levels of meaning and purpose in the second half—the *best* half—of life.

In my book, *Scaling Up: How a Few Companies Make It...and Why the Rest Don't*, I wrote, "Goals without routines are wishes; routines without goals are aimless. The most successful people have a clear vision and the disciplines (routines) to make it a reality." John's unique Legacy Map process helps you do just that! His powerful, life-focusing tool helps you reach meaningful goals, defy stereotypes, and leave a lasting legacy.

Buckminster Fuller once wrote, "If you want to teach people a new way of thinking, don't bother trying to teach them. Instead, give them a tool, the use of which will lead to new ways of thinking." The Legacy Map is the purpose-built tool you need to align your highest priorities with goals and daily routines to make them a reality.

I think the future is bright. Very bright. But you need to be ready. *Replace Retirement: Living Your Legacy in the Exponential Age* contains navigational aids and real-life examples to chart an amazing course that will impact you, your family, and the world.

John's passion is helping people navigate what success looks like at every life stage. And he's especially gifted at helping folks map out their own future. So jump in, read on, and discover how you and I can contribute enormous value at any age.

# PREFACE

Hate waiting in line at the airport?

Tired of cramped seats and crying babies?

I can tell you from experience, flying by private jet is a lot more fun. You feel like a rock star, you're treated like royalty, and they never lose your luggage.

But I'm getting ahead of myself. My story didn't begin by riding in Citation jets and eating at five-star restaurants. I rose up quickly, made some good and bad choices, and got back on track later in life.

As a young man, I achieved significant wealth. The trappings of success came easily. I had status and influence. By age 40, I had attained what most consider the American dream and found that it did not satisfy. From the outside, it looked like I'd won the lotto of life. But inside, I longed for a more meaningful and intentional future. How I discovered and defined a second-half life of purpose, impact, and lasting significance inspired me to write this book.

Today, at age 60, I'm co-owner of two companies and have equity in several others. But my primary identity and time commitment are focused on coaching a unique process I helped create for business owners called The CEO Advantage™.

As a business coach and advisor, I work with an elite cadre of successful executives who wish to hone their leadership skills and leverage their accomplishments. To help them, I developed a tool called The Legacy Map™. With my assistance, clients use it to create a personalized plan for identifying, monitoring, and living out their goals.

While The CEO Advantage was designed to help a *team,* The Legacy Map was designed to help *individual leaders* create a legacy—professionally and personally. Their customized "road map" details a daily path through life that aligns and measures progress while ensuring it ends at a purposeful destination.

Then one day it hit me: *What if EVERYBODY could do what my clients were doing? What if anyone over 50 could use the same Legacy Map principles to reach their most important life goals?*

By making the Legacy Map widely available, I could challenge my generation —65 million Baby Boomers—to envision their second-half life as a time of exponential impact and abundance. You're holding the results of that decision in your hand.

———

Today, 10,000 Americans will hit 65.

That transition will go on every day for roughly the next 20 years. Most of those people have little or no idea what they'll do over their next 30 or 40 years.

In light of this uncertainty, I challenge Baby Boomers to be proactive with a bold plan: *Replace retirement with intentional living.*

Exactly what that looks like is different for each person. But my advice for anyone nearing retirement age is the same: don't slow down. In fact, accelerate your pace of living and create a second-half of value, purpose, and meaning.

If properly motivated, this group can be a game changer for our society and economy. Utilizing their skills can unleash an outpouring of entrepreneurship and nonprofit community service—all in the name of personal freedom.

It's time to *reimagine* our futures and *rededicate* ourselves to using our hard-earned wisdom for the next generation's benefit. Hopefully, we can live such a powerful second-half life that Millennials and beyond will want to imitate us.

That's why I'm asking Baby Boomers to skip retirement, stay in the game, and apply, to their second half of life, the same genius for innovation and job creation that made them the wealthiest generation in history.

Instead of fading away, Boomers can become the most sought-after assets of a changing demographic landscape. As our population becomes majority gray, some of us will have to play catch-up with new technologies. And some of us will need to re-think our concept of aging. But here's the upside—we have more skills, education, and job experience than any prior group our age ever dreamed of.

Clearly there are challenges with aging. But the attitude that will carry us is the same one that has historically carried Americans through global conflicts, natural disasters, and economic downturns—*perseverance.*

"Finishing well" despite difficulty was the cornerstone of our parents' era. That is a core value we want—and need—to pass on to our children. How?

- By shifting our retirement paradigm from leisure to learning

- By viewing our second half as the better half

- By caring for our mind, body, and spirit

- By dedicating our decades of experience to helping others

- By role-modeling a fully engaged life to younger generations

Aging is inevitable.

Quitting is not.

America's "Greatest Generation" was known not only for their tenacity and grit, but also for demonstrating unprecedented entrepreneurship and creativity. And in many ways, we're still standing on their shoulders. Let's honor their example by becoming self-sustaining dynamos that crush every stereotype about retirement-age adults.

> *"Ask yourself what is really important and then have the courage to build your life around your answer."*
>
> —UNKNOWN

# THE EXPONENTIAL AGE

## EMBRACING ACCELERATING CHANGE IN THE MOST AMAZING TIME IN HISTORY TO BE ALIVE

*"Our intuition about the future is linear. But the reality of information technology is exponential, and that makes a profound difference. If I take 30 steps linearly, I get to 30. If I take 30 steps exponentially, I get to a billion."*

—RAY KURZWEIL

*"The best way to predict the future is to create it."*

—ABRAHAM LINCOLN

# What Can You Learn from a Taxi Ride?

My recent experience with an airport cab driver underscores the huge dividing line being caused *right now* by the Exponential Age.

Perhaps this book is your first in-depth exposure to exponential thinking. Or perhaps like me, you've been following this trend closely.

We are living in exponential times, but we grew up in a linear world. As Boomers, we've been ingrained with linear thinking through education, business, and government models—virtually every system and process. Based on our past, we expect things to move on a fairly linear path. Many of my high-achieving readers have excelled at this linear game. Your success with this way of thinking is why some of you are running businesses that drive our economy. Nevertheless, the fact is that a linear way of thinking is impeding your opportunity for growth.

In the words of Marshall Goldsmith's all-too-true book title, *What Got You Here Won't Get You There.*

This book and my Legacy Map tool are designed to introduce a new way of looking at the world (and our individual futures) through an exponential lens—to train our linear brains to spot trends, insights, and opportunities.

We are at the most exciting time in history for those willing to learn and change. If not, we'll be like the cab driver who picked me up at the Grand Rapids airport this spring. It was a beautiful Sunday night with one of those gorgeous Lake Michigan sunsets. I got in the cab and told the driver I was just going to the Courtyard hotel. That's an eight-minute ride. The driver told me he'd been waiting at the airport over two hours for his first fare—me. He went on to say how disappointed he was to be dropping me only a few miles away. I'd be his last fare of the night, because he wanted to see his children before bedtime and reclaim some of his lost evening.

As I parted, I gave him a generous tip for such a short ride. But I didn't have the heart to give him the tip he *really* needed. His business has been irreparably disrupted by exponential thinking in the form of Uber—and, ultimately, autonomous cars.

Like all of us, he needed to hear that his old linear way of life was never returning. My cab driver was disrupted by technology and societal evolution, and he never saw it coming.

To succeed in our second half, we need to ensure this doesn't happen to us.

Ready or not, here comes the future.

Today's commerce is being fueled by a new breed of risk-takers—a group of innovators leading the charge not just in business, but in fighting poverty, addressing injustice, and driving innovations that benefit everyone.

Maybe you're on board with that. And maybe you're not.

Perhaps you'd rather sit this one out. *After all*, you think, *I've worked hard. I've won my race.* It's tempting to assume, *Now's the time for winding down and lying low. Let someone else push the envelope. Count me out.*

That's not only myopic, it's impractical.

You can embrace change or you can ignore it. But you can't avoid it. Sticking your head in the sand won't prevent change. It will only diminish the benefits we might attain by being prepared.

Somebody said, "The future has a funny way of sneaking up on you. You don't notice it's here until you're soaking in it."

Or in this case, bobbing around in it.

Fortunately, we can do more than just tread water. We can go surfing.

This section is about the exponential change that's transforming our world even as you read this...a change that can be bewildering or empowering.

# Creating a Legacy in the Exponential Age.

Your future is going to have one of two radically different outcomes based on how you adapt to the tsunami of change that's underway and picking up speed at a rate you can hardly imagine. At an *exponential* rate.

"If you don't design your own life plan, chances are you'll fall into someone else's. And guess what they have planned for you? Not much."

That's according to the late Jim Rohn, and I couldn't agree more.

The Exponential Age is powered by exponentially accelerating technologies. Two *simultaneous revolutions* are emerging at lightning speed:

- **Technology.** Older Americans with the right mindset can take advantage of exponential growth in communications and technology that previous generations couldn't imagine. Opportunities for seniors to thrive financially and start new enterprises are at an all-time high—and growing by the day.

- **Demographics.** You're likely to live significantly longer than you might think. Life expectancy is increasing by two years every decade with no signs of slowing. Our generation is poised to benefit from exponential growth in medicine and geriatrics that will push our life span past triple digits.

Is that an overstatement? Quite the opposite. A study in *The Lancet* calls the imminent gain of 30 years in life expectancy for first-world populations "one of the most important accomplishments of the twentieth century."

"If people knew they would live to be 100, they might want to organize their lives very differently," says Professor James Vaupel, co-author of *The Lancet* study.

That's what this book is about—organizing your life *differently* in light of the technological and demographic revolutions.

This revolution didn't start with a couple of nerds named Gates and

Jobs. It's been a long time coming. Need proof? Just ask a pair of bicycle builders from Dayton, Ohio.

In my life, I've flown in everything from private jets to the Concorde. Most of the time, I thought nothing of it. But then it hit me. The history of aviation is *based* on exponential growth:

- In 1783, the Montgolfier brothers launched the first hot-air balloon with human passengers.

- In 1903, Orville Wright flew the first powered aircraft. His flight lasted 12 seconds and covered 120 feet.

- In 1969, Neil Armstrong walked on the moon. Apollo 11's flight lasted eight days and covered 935,054 miles.

That's exponential growth. From the beginning of recorded history, it took 6,000 years for man to defy gravity in a balloon. Then, only 120 more years to fly an airplane. Then, a mere 66 more to reach the moon.

But the progression gets even wilder. Just eight years after "one small step for man," NASA sent a probe to explore our entire solar system.

In 1977, Voyager 1 was launched to study Jupiter, Uranus, and the outer solar system. Almost 40 years later, it's still whizzing along at 38,000 mph and has totally blown past Pluto. In fact, it's already 11.7 billion miles from Earth in deep interstellar space. Then it will orbit inside the Milky Way galaxy, maybe forever.

That's a long way from Kitty Hawk, North Carolina.

# An Uncertain, Wavy, Creeping Flight.

Like most advances in human history, the story of manned flight follows the classic exponential curve. As you move along the curve—upward and to the right—things start out very slow (almost horizontally) and then pick up speed at enormously fast rates (almost vertically).

The birth of flight proves how agonizingly slow that first phase can be! For all of you who are wondering if the great idea that's been bouncing around in your brain for years is worth anything, take heart from the humble beginnings of the pioneers of flight.

In *The Wright Brothers*, David McCullough reveals the staggering odds the brothers faced. Wilbur and Orville's 605-pound invention—nicknamed the "Flyer"—lifted off the sand dunes of North Carolina in 1903. It stayed airborne just long enough to make history.

That's the part we all know. What's less well-known is how little support they had. The US government basically ignored the Wrights. So did investors. Even the American media paid little or no attention.

The odds were stacked against them from the start. They had no formal training as engineers. They had no funding. They had no stockholders, no venture capitalists, no financial backers. They supported themselves and their experiments solely on income generated from their bicycle shop in Ohio.

Instead of attending university, they studied birds, read books, and took a swing at building a glider. After that, they scraped together a few dollars and built a motor-powered aircraft. The windy North Carolina sand dunes were their test lab.

McCullough reports that skepticism was intense. Many experts rejected even the possibility of powered flight. Only *five* people were on hand to watch the historic first flight. In the understatement of the century, Orville described his history-making achievement as "an uncertain, wavy, creeping sort of a flight at best."

But it was enough to spur the bike mechanics to fly higher, faster, and farther.

In 1908, the brothers and their assistants took the fragile Flyer to France. In front of an adoring press, Wilbur cracked off a test flight lasting almost two minutes.

Word spread like wildfire. It spread exponentially.

## LEAVE A LEGACY

Lack of experience can't hold you back. Your personal experiences can lead to universal applications. Jeffrey Nash was a men's clothing salesman who made a great deal of money for his employers, but he always wanted a business of his own. Inspiration struck one day in 2008 when he was at a soccer game with his granddaughters. He saw a young mother teaching her baby to walk. She was hunched over uncomfortably, and she would have to yank on the toddler's arms if it started to fall. He invented the "Juppy"—a long, cloth sling that keeps the child upright without the parent having to pull on the child's arms. After running it through initial tests with customers, he connected with a manufacturer. Nash has since sold $500,000 worth of his Juppy Baby Walkers, making an average of $80,000 a year.

By 1909, the brothers were arguably the most famous men in the world, sought out by politicians, royal families, and wealthy businessmen. Reporters and cheering crowds flocked to see them fly. The brothers were invited to the White House by President Taft. The city of Dayton threw a lavish homecoming.

Funded and famous beyond his dreams, Wilbur made more news by circling the Statue of Liberty and making a 33-minute flight along the Hudson River's crowded skyline. In roughly six years, they went from an audience of five at Kitty Hawk to over a million viewers in Manhattan. That's *exponential* growth.

Why is any of this important? Because many of you are the Wright brothers of today. You are current (or soon-to-be) second-half entrepreneurs. Like the Wright brothers, you are risk-takers. But to reach the next level, you'll need to be thinking *exponentially.* Your big idea may seem strange to those stuck in the linear paradigm. Peers, media, and even friends may doubt your credibility.

That's okay. The future belongs to dreamers who believe outrageous things like the notion of men flying like birds. As the saying goes, "May you have ideas so big they grow wings."

## The World Is Waiting for Your Ideas.

I encourage you to dream big.

But don't expect everyone to rally around you with encouragement. Remember, it was the *French* who started the ball rolling for the Wright brothers. In today's flat earth economy, the "French" might be crowdfunding or open-source sharing or networking with investors from around the globe.

If you're going to make an impact (and bring about the next generation of solutions), you'll need to be flexible, improvisational, and make use of new technologies. That's why the Wright brothers built their own wind tunnel.

Don't rely on the government.

Don't rely on what's worked in the past.

The Wrights succeeded because of their self-directed learning. They were not confined by conventional ways of thinking and solving problems. Their competitors were products of traditional practices. Orville and Wilbur's innovations—like "wing warping" for lateral control—came from outside the box.

Our generation has a similar challenge.

Boomers came of age in a linear world. Our education system was intentionally developed to support economic success in the Industrial Age. The problem-solving strategies and business philosophies we learned were based on (1) utilizing scarce, limited resources and (2) achieving predictable, linear growth.

This linear thinking worked for decades, but it won't carry us into the burgeoning Exponential Age. Like the Wrights, we need to develop a new perspective.

Change is accelerating in scale and speed. There are an infinite number of discoveries and breakthroughs waiting to be made by second-halfers. Let's scale up the vision of our futures to match this era of unprecedented opportunity.

Above all, don't ever think we've run out of things to invent or new ways to make money. Consider these epic miscalculations:

> *"Television won't be able to hold onto any market it captures after the first six months. People will soon get tired of staring at a plywood box every night."*
>
> —DARRYL ZANUCK, EXECUTIVE AT 20ᵀᴴ CENTURY FOX

> *"I think there is a world market for maybe five computers."*
>
> —THOMAS WATSON, PRESIDENT OF IBM

> *"There is no reason anyone would want a computer in their home."*
>
> —KEN OLSEN, COFOUNDER OF
> DIGITAL EQUIPMENT CORPORATION

One generation ago, no one had a smartphone in their pocket, an ATM card in their wallet, or a navigation system in their car. Two generations ago, no one had color TV, central air, or power steering.

As I said, there are an infinite number of discoveries and breakthroughs waiting to be made. If you doubt it, ask Ray Kurzweil.

At 70, Kurzweil is the world's best-known futurist. For decades, he's successfully predicted exponential growth with uncanny accuracy. Now he foresees breakthroughs so radical they might surprise even the intrepid Wright brothers. "Once we figured out the secret to flight—the subtle scientific principles—we created the world of aviation. Once we can build and create (artificial) intelligence that doesn't have the limitations of our brain, there is *nothing* it can't do."

In 2009, Kurzweil told *Rolling Stone*, "As computer intelligence surpasses that of humans, machines will make smarter and smarter versions of themselves—without any help from us."

That's not science fiction, that's the exponential power of technology.

On an average day, over eight million people fly. The International Air Transport Association reports that airlines welcomed 3.6 billion passengers in 2016.

And it all started with Orville's 12-second solo flight.

Be ready to challenge your linear assumptions to get your dream off the ground (pun intended).

# Understanding Exponential Growth.

Simply put, exponential growth means the *rate of change* increases over time; that is, the *rate of growth* becomes faster as time passes. It's true of viruses (think influenza), populations (think India), and the national debt (think Washington)!

Speaking of money, want to double yours? At first, the idea of such acceleration may be scary, but you should think instead of how you can use its powers on your behalf. Or, viewed another way, think of how it could increase the number of people you could help. Even the *money* from your great ideas could experience exponential growth.

Fortunes have been made by employing a facet of exponential growth we all know as compound interest. If you remember Econ 101, compounding simply means taking the interest you earn on an investment and adding it to the principal so the interest also earns interest—exponentially.

The quick-and-dirty math is that at a 12 percent return, you double your initial investment every six years. At a more realistic 6 percent rate of return, your money doubles in 12 years. That's exponential growth, pure and simple.

Another explanation is found in this classic riddle: A wealthy family agrees to pay their son for doing chores around the house. As compensation, he's offered two choices. Plan A is a flat fee of $1,000,000. In Plan B, they will give him one penny the first day, two pennies the second day, four pennies the third, eight pennies the fourth, and continue doubling the previous day's pay for one entire month.

I hope you chose Plan B because it totals $20,474,836.

Okay, so high interest rates don't grow on trees. And nobody gets a $1M allowance. But the principle of exponential growth applies to countless other areas of life, from medicine to technology to entertainment.

Remember George Jetson and his flying car? On his radio broadcast, financial advisor Ric Edelman predicted we'll likely see that Jetson scenario in our lifetime. (Flying cars first appeared on the cover of *Popular Mechanics* in 1931.) When George arrived at work, he folded his car into his briefcase instead of parking. With autonomous cars coming, we won't have to park at all—our vehicles will drop us off and continue on their own to carry others or be swapped around in a giant pool of shared vehicles.

Trouble keeping the house tidy? Jane Jetson had Rosie the robot maid to help with little Elroy. Nice. But today's robotic vacuum cleaners and "super-smart" computerized homes are catching up quick.

Edelman says what is most shocking is just how *close* we are to the future dreamed up by Hanna-Barbera in 1962. It's the *speed* that exponential technology is becoming reality that's going to take most people by surprise.

Visionary Ray Kurzweil wrote prophetically about what he dubbed the Law of Accelerating Change (which would later morph into his Laws of Accelerating Returns) way back in 2001: "An analysis of the history of technology shows that technological change is exponential, contrary to the common-sense 'intuitive linear' view. So we won't experience 100 years of progress in the twenty-first century—it will be more like 20,000 years of progress (at today's rate)... There's even exponential growth in the rate of exponential growth."

For early man, breakthroughs like stone tools, portable fire, and the wheel took tens of thousands of years. Centuries went by with virtually no technological progress. Then, says Kurzweil, it began ramping up. "In the nineteenth century, we saw more technological change than in the nine centuries preceding it. Then in the first twenty years of the twentieth century, we saw more advancement than in all of the nineteenth century. Now, paradigm shifts occur in only a few years' time."

If that sounds far-fetched, consider the internet. Its ancestor was designed in the 1980s to connect regional military and academic networks. By the early 1990s, it was opened up for commercial use. In 1995, it had 16 million users. By 2000, it had 361 million users.

By 2005, it had over a billion users. By 2010, it had nearly 2 billion users. By 2016, there were 3.5 billion users online!

All that growth took only 20 years. And with developing nations coming online, it's accelerating at an even faster pace. A real-time counter on a site called *internetlivestats.com* shows millions of new users connecting as numbers flash by at a breathtaking rate.

But even that's on the verge of sounding out-of-date.

As of this writing, we're getting tantalizingly close to "the super-connected, ultra-fast, 5G world that tech companies have been promising." According to Karissa Bell, "Most of us have never experienced anything close to speeds that fast." In her article, "5 Things to Know About 5G," Bell says the fastest 4G download speeds in the US top out around 19 megabits per second. "5G, by comparison, promises *gigabit* speeds." That's at least 1,000 times faster.

But 5G isn't just about ultra-fast data *connection*, it's about exponentially higher *capacity*—to power technology for self-driving cars, robotics, consumer tech, virtual reality, and more. Experts predict deployment by 2020.

## LEAVE A LEGACY

Do you sometimes feel left out of all the activity swirling around you? You're probably not going to join a company developing phone apps anytime soon, but you *can* learn what you need for your own purposes. You don't even have to commit to driving to a community college a few nights a week. You can learn a tremendous amount right at home. According to a Pew Research Center poll, 80 percent of American adults don't know about the booming new trend in online learning. Massive open online courses (MOOCs) are now being offered by universities and companies all over the world. How to find them? Try Coursera or Khan Academy. They both offer courses online for anyone to take, for free. Or check out *edx.org* for courses with costs under $100. When you do, you'll be enjoying another side benefit of exponential growth created by the internet.

At the same time, an explosion of new internet networks will unleash what Peter Diamandis calls "global ubiquitous connectivity." He says this exponential internet growth is on track to produce four billion new users by 2025—on a blazing fast 5G infrastructure we can barely imagine. That's four billion new consumers, creators, and entrepreneurs clamoring to jump in and drive the global economy upwards by trillions of dollars.

We're living in the Exponential Age, and it's only the beginning. Just 15 years ago, Kurzweil wrote: "Within a few decades, machine intelligence will surpass human intelligence, leading to The Singularity—technological change so rapid and profound it represents a rupture in the fabric of human history. The implications include the merger of biological and non-biological intelligence, immortal software-based humans, and ultra-high levels of intelligence that expand...at the speed of light."

That's mind-blowing.

But then so was the sight of a horseless carriage in 1768. It was invented in France by Nicolas-Joseph Cugnot, who used steam to power the world's first self-propelled mechanical vehicle.

It took another 118 years before Karl Benz introduced the first gasoline-powered automobile in 1886.

By 1996—just 100 years later—there were 500 million vehicles on the road. By 2010, there were one billion.

Again, exponential growth.

I mention cars because I'm based in the Detroit area, the Motor City. And we love our wheels. I like nothing better than to tour the back roads in my Tahoe. But if you have a child or grandchild who's five years old, they may *never drive a car*. Self-driving autos are here, and within 10 to 15 years, they'll be the norm.

Can you get your head around that?

They've been worked on since the 1970s, but technology is accelerating *exponentially*. A report in *The Wall Street Journal* says autonomous cars could eliminate 90 percent of crashes in the US and save $190 billion a year on damage and injuries.

Here's the cool part—when technology moves from linear to exponential, the applications spread like wildfire and millions benefit from the collateral. A profusion of driverless technologies has already trickled down into standard vehicles in features like adaptive cruise control, lane departure prevention, collision avoidance, and more.

# Focusing on Tomorrow.

The epicenter for futurists is Singularity University, founded in 2008 near San Francisco. I've met with the school's cofounders, Peter Diamandis and Ray Kurzweil, and attended their pilot program for an annual event now known as Abundance 360.

This renowned think tank tracks and nurtures the life-altering shifts that are affecting society, including nanotechnology, robotics, and big data. These and other areas of radical transformation—like biomechanics and genetic engineering—will extend our life span, improve global standards of living, and bring fundamental changes in every aspect of life:

- **Nanotechnology**. Essentially the manipulation of individual atoms and molecules, this science deals with dimensions of less than 100 nanometers. In case you missed *Honey, I Shrunk the Kids*, a nanometer is one-billionth of a meter. That's how much your fingernail grows in one second. Engineers are designing and building machines so small they're invisible with a standard microscope.

- **Medicine**. Imagine machines so tiny they float through your bloodstream and repair damaged cells. (The 1966 sci-fi movie *Fantastic Voyage* predicted this.) Now imagine a computer implanted inside your brain that allows networks to exchange information—direct from one mind to another. Neurochemistry and experimental psychology are quickly unraveling brain structure and function.

- **Big data and analytics**. Immense amounts of complex data are being acquired. This tech can access, manage, manipulate, and analyze it. What can big data do? Track and predict weather. Show societal trends. Analyze consumer behavior. Think of the data Target or Walmart collects daily from millions of transactions.

- **Energy and environment**. Alternative, renewable energy from sun, wind, water, and batteries. Solar will likely emerge the winner once the issues of storage and transfer are solved. The development of environmental management systems driven by big data may soon control the weather and help eliminate famine, alter destructive climate patterns, and avert natural disasters.

- **Robotics**. Over the next 10 to 15 years, half the jobs in this world may be replaced by robots. Any mechanized, repeatable task that is currently done by a human can soon be done by a robot. Think of the freedom that will provide by getting rid of the drudgery—but also think of the massive disruption and unemployment among unskilled workers.

- **3-D Printing**. Every day, industries are making physical objects from digital models. Doctors are even 3-D "printing" living tissue and human organs that will transform surgical replacements. And scientists are working on 4-D printing—where a 3-D object morphs due to a change in temperature, light, or humidity. Think of *Transformers*. That's 4-D printing. The "fourth D" is time.

- **Bioinformatics**. If you wear a Fitbit wristband, you're already adapting to this technology. Wearable devices that track your body's biometrics through an array of sensors can check heart rate, steps taken, and amount of REM sleep. Upload it to your smartphone and you can track your performance or send it to your physician. With crowdsourcing, entire populations may soon be tracked.

- **Financial services**. Nontraditional funding sources and platforms for commerce are barging in. Think digital currencies—like the bitcoin—and you'll have an idea of how the storing and transferring of money is going to look in the near future. It may be vastly different than cash or even debit and credit cards.

# Moore's Exponential Future.

There's an old joke about personal computers. You buy a brand-new computer, take it home, and unpack it. In the bottom of the box, there's an ad for a new model that makes yours obsolete.

If that's happened to you, blame Moore's Law.

Back in 1965, Gordon Moore, cofounder of Intel, observed that the number of transistors per chip had doubled every year since the integrated circuit was invented. Moore predicted this trend would continue. Today, 50 years later, data density still doubles about every 18 months. Most experts, including Moore himself, expect the trend to hold for at least another 25 years and beyond.

Moore saw that the newly invented electronic chips were improving at an exponential rate. He plotted the price and performance points on a graph and made a projection so bold that it sounded like science fiction.

At first, his graph rose slowly. As Rich Karlgaard points out in *Team Genius: The New Science of High-Performing Organizations*, Moore's projection curve was very shallow until about 2005. Yet, even along that flat curve, we find the births of the microprocessor, the digital calculator, personal computers, the internet, robotics, the smartphone, and e-commerce. Karlgaard says, "If the entire digital age occurred in the foothills, what's going to happen now that we're entering the Himalayas?"

To give a framework for understanding how Moore's Law is affecting our economy and future, authors Peter Diamandis and Steven Kotler wrote *Bold: How to Go Big, Create Wealth and Impact the World*. (This 2015 book is a follow-up to their 2012 work, *Abundance: The Future Is Better Than You Think*.)

Futurists like Diamandis and Kotler see billion-dollar opportunities behind the world's biggest problems—poverty, preventable diseases, lack of clean water, and even the scourge of aging. They demonstrate how Moore's Law has unleashed exponential technologies that are already resulting in advances like cleaner power, safer vehicles, and new medicines.

Former executive director of Singularity University, Salim Ismail, explains why this quantum leap is occurring. In his 2014 book, *Exponential Organizations*, he writes, "That steady, extraordinary, and seemingly impossible pace led futurist Ray Kurzweil, who has studied this phenomenon for 30 years, to make four signature observations." They are:

1. The doubling pattern identified by Gordon Moore in integrated circuits applies to any information technology.

2. The driver fueling this is information. Once any technology or industry becomes information enabled, its price/performance begins doubling annually.

3. Once the doubling pattern starts, it doesn't stop. We use current computers to design faster computers, which then build faster computers, and so on.

4. Current technologies following this trajectory include artificial intelligence, robotics, biotech and bioinformatics, neuroscience, data science, 3-D printing, energy, nanotechnology, and medicine.

Ismail sums it up, "Never in human history have we seen so many technologies moving at such a pace."

Think about how Moore's Law and Kurzweil's principles will radically affect medicine *alone*. If medical knowledge and technology is doubling every year, we're on the brink of solving killers like stroke and heart disease. In the near future, we'll move from "reactive" (healing) medicine to "proactive" (preventive) medicine. By analyzing our genome sequencing and tracking our physiology, doctors may soon predict and neutralize threats like cancer or diabetes, prescribing diets and regimens tailored to our unique vulnerabilities.

Bottom line? Much longer life expectancy with much healthier lives.

People living to 100-plus will be normal, not an anomaly. As my friend and mentor, Dr. Peter Diamandis, often says, "100 is the new 60." And he backs it up with updated reports on breakthroughs in genomics and cutting-edge research. (I encourage you to subscribe to his newsletter and blog at *diamandis.com*.)

But all those extra years must be planned for.

Consider this a friendly wakeup call for any and all of us who still think tomorrow is going to resemble today. Because it won't.

## LEAVE A LEGACY

What marks the Baby Boomer generation? The ability to work hard to achieve a goal. There's no reason you can't roll up your sleeves and join the tech world. Regardless of age or background. After 20 years as a research physicist for DuPont, Gillian Reynolds-Titko was laid off. She began looking for a new job. But rather than stay on her career path, she decided to learn a new skill—*programming*. She didn't know a thing about it, so she started taking free online courses, watching videos, and reading books. That wasn't good enough, so she signed up for an intense 12-week boot camp course to learn. Afterward, she got a job as an IT business analyst for JPMorgan Chase. Still, it wasn't easy. She had to work at it. She said, "See if it's something you really want to do. If it is, commit to it, because it's going to take a lot of work to make the change."

# David (the Disrupter) and Goliath.

I admit it. I like to go fast and take risks.

I ride my dirt bike up to 1,000 off-road miles per year. And I ride my snowmobile 7,000 to 10,000 miles per winter (that's *not* a typo).

Another one of my motorized passions is my personal watercraft. It's a Sea-Doo RXP with 260 horsepower. It can outrun or outmaneuver just about anything on the water.

When you're small and nimble like my Sea-Doo (or a tiny start-up company), changing direction is easy. But what if my ride was over a quarter-mile long?

The largest ship in the world is a supertanker owned by Shell. Called the *Prelude*, it's 1,601 feet long—or 150 feet longer than the Empire State Building is high. Because of their enormous momentum, it takes a fully loaded tanker about 20 minutes and over 5.5 miles to stop. Changing course is agonizingly slow—nearly 15 minutes to make a U-turn, with a turning circle of over two miles.

My point is obvious: bigger ships (and organizations) are slower. Less responsive. More *linear*. In fact, rapid change is nearly impossible for tankers *and* traditional corporations, institutions, or governments to implement—or survive.

That makes traditional "linear" businesses extremely vulnerable to disruption by lean and mean competitors operating out of the "exponential" matrix.

And these disrupters are often post-retirement-age citizens. In 2017, 94-year-old John Goodenough (co-inventor of the lithium-ion battery) developed the first all-solid-state battery cells that could lead to safer, faster-charging, longer-lasting rechargeable batteries for handheld mobile devices, electric cars, and stationary energy storage.

Goodenough is only one of a million unlikely success stories of nonlinear, web-driven, technology-based innovators changing the landscape.

Industrial monoliths cannot deal or compete with *wunderkinds* (like you) popping up all over the globe. With access to big data and exponential technology, anyone of any age (including you) in any culture has the potential to disrupt a blue-chip company.

Don't believe it? A study from the School of Business at Washington University estimates 40 percent of today's Fortune 500 companies on the S&P 500 will no longer exist in 10 years. Peter Diamandis adds, "If you started a company in the 1920s on the S&P 500, you had a 67-year run rate before someone disrupted you. Today, you've got 15 years. And that rate is shrinking."

Watching today's fast-rising entrepreneurs (exponential) battle the traditional business models (linear) is a lot like watching a personal watercraft outmaneuver a slow-moving supertanker.

Founded in 2008, Airbnb (as in "bed and breakfast") disrupted the hospitality industry by enabling travelers to rent space in private homes directly from residents. *Top Hotel News* reports it "now has 4 million listings in 191 countries across the globe." Airbnb has "more options listed than the top five hotel brands combined." That includes Marriott, Hilton, Hyatt, Wyndham, and InterContinental. And it just keeps growing.

Founded in 2009, Uber converts private autos into taxis. Love it or hate it, the scrappy newcomer was valued at $68 billion in 2017—despite having virtually no physical assets or payroll employees.

Based in San Francisco, Uber allows consumers with smartphones to submit a trip request that's routed to Uber drivers who use their own cars—in over 60 countries and forty cities worldwide.

Untold others have copied Uber's business model for stripped-down, on-demand services. This phenomenon is known as "Uberification." For whatever you need, just hit an app on your smartphone and it magically shows up. From housekeeping to bookkeeping, thousands of new virtual businesses are disrupting the status quo and displacing brick-and-mortar establishments. At an exponential rate.

This trend to an on-demand economy is a wake-up call that the world is changing rapidly. My point? Second-halfers can apply the same principles of exponential growth that *business* is using to plan and create their own *personal* futures!

———

For many in my generation, success was our fundamental goal. It meant picking the right college, right career, right spouse, right neighborhood. Whether it was success in our jobs or in our relationships, we worked hard at...well, *everything*. And it was pretty exhilarating striving for all that success.

But in reality, the definition of success can change with differing perspectives. Winston Churchill defined it as "the ability to go from one failure to another with no loss of enthusiasm."

Albert Schweitzer noted, "Success is not the key to happiness. Happiness is the key to success. If you love what you are doing, you will be successful." That's the kind of second-half success I'm describing. And it's the kind that inspires Tommy Caldwell to reach higher. Caldwell is considered the greatest rock climber of all time. (If you Google his videos, get ready for vertigo.)

Many of Caldwell's big-wall free climbs are so extreme that the routes are never repeated. Author Jim Collins caught up with Caldwell while he was preparing for a pioneer ascent up an unconquered face of El Capitan in Yosemite. Collins asked the elite climber about failing, "How will you feel if you don't succeed?"

Caldwell replied, "Every step of the way is making me grow and making me stronger and making every other climb look relatively easy. And if I don't succeed, then I've given a gift to future generations. I've pointed the way for them."

That's what we need to do. Push ourselves. Stick our necks out. Point the way for future generations. We might reach the top; we might slip and fall. But either way, we will be the inspiration future generations can use to make the summit.

## Exponentially Fit.

Every morning, I perform a ritual consisting of four things: I pray, write in my blog or journal, read from great books, and exercise. That usually means 60 push-ups, 100 crunches, and 45 squats (broken up into sets—I'm not a Navy SEAL). I also do curls and ride a stationary bike on alternate days.

What's the point of this discipline?

I'm 60 years old. And to be honest, I don't see a big change yet. I don't look or feel radically different than most men my age. But I'm not in it for the short run. I'm in for the full 103 years (if that sounds odd, I'll explain later).

When I'm 65, I'll be noticeably ahead of my peer group. I'll be slimmer, healthier, smarter, and less grumpy. At 75, the gap will be even more pronounced. I'll be more active, more engaged, and more energetic than my peers. At 85, I'll stand out in a crowd. At 95, even more.

So not only do I have an exceptional quality of life today, but exercising my mind, body, and spirit will pay off exponentially in the future.

Same for you, if you'll join me. But you have to think *long term*.

Remember how exponential growth works. Both in technology and in our personal lives, a curve can start deceptively flat but then rises very quickly. Just like Moore's Law, the benefit curve of my morning ritual is starting out slow and flat but will ramp up faster and steeper as years go by.

There's an old saying: "The best time to start a fitness program is 10 years ago. The second-best time is today." That maxim also applies to every challenge in this book. Whether you're 40 or 80, get started now and watch the principles of exponential growth and intentional living transform everything.

> "Look to the future because that's where you'll spend the rest of your life."
>
> —GEORGE BURNS, ENTERTAINER AND CENTENARIAN

# LIVE LONG AND PROSPER

## ABSOLUTE PROOF THE SECOND HALF OF LIFE CAN BE RIDICULOUSLY BETTER THAN THE FIRST

"Age is an issue of mind over matter. If you don't mind, it doesn't matter."

—MARK TWAIN

"Of all the self-fulfilling prophecies of our culture, the assumption that aging means decline and poor health is probably the deadliest."

—MARILYN FERGUSON

# Rock and Roll Never Forgets.

*"Encore! Encore! Encore!"*

The man in the spotlight lifted his guitar above his head and waved to the noisy crowd. For three hours, he had played song after song with an intensity that kept 20,000 fans on their feet. From the stage to the rafters, Detroit's Joe Louis Arena reverberated with rock anthems, pyrotechnics, and the shouts of people lucky enough to get tickets to the sold-out tour.

The energetic rock star played and sang 38 hit songs with no intermission.

Then he did three encores.

The show was flawless, the pace was relentless.

Here's the surprise: the rocker was 75 years old.

For years, I've been teaching that second-halfers can add enormous value for themselves and others, regardless of age or societal norms. Now I can rest my case. Sir Paul McCartney proved me right as three generations of music lovers screamed their (young and old) heads off with joy and gratitude.

McCartney demonstrates it's possible to cross demographic and cultural barriers when you use your gifts and talents past retirement age. Fans of all ages continue to pack out his shows in Europe, Asia, South America, and beyond.

I'd say the lad from Liverpool is a poster child for *replacing retirement with intentional living.*

McCartney's popularity and revenue are classic examples of the exponential curve in action. In 1960, he played for 100 people in Liverpool. In 1965, he played for 55,000 at New York's Shea Stadium. In 2008, he played for 350,000 in Kiev's Independence Square. That's exponential.

And his income is on the same up-and-to-the-right curve. McCartney recently played three nights at the Tokyo Dome and 146,845 people showed up. In that city alone, he grossed $24 million. At the time of this writing, Sir Paul's "Out There" tour has taken in over $300 million and climbing.

Here's a textbook example: In 1964, The Beatles earned just $10,000 for all three appearances on *The Ed Sullivan Show* (their debut drew a record 73-million viewers). In 2012, the TV show *Mad Men* paid $250,000 for the rights to use *one* Lennon-McCartney song ("Tomorrow Never Knows") in a *single* episode.

Variations on that kind of trajectory—from modest beginnings to meteoric rise—are being repeated daily in this Exponential Age we're blessed to live in.

## A Birthday to Remember.

On June 18, 2006, Paul McCartney turned 64.

Why was that significant?

I'm guessing you're already humming the answer.

Although the subject of "When I'm Sixty-Four" is aging, McCartney composed it on the family piano as a teenager. He used to perform it in the local Cavern Club when the Beatles were known as The Quarrymen. The song was dusted off and recorded in December 1966 (the year McCartney's father turned 64) for the seminal album, *Sgt. Pepper's Lonely Hearts Club Band.*

The lyrics focus on a young man nervously looking toward his own old age: "When I get older, losing my hair, many years from now." Sung to his lover, it frames his pessimistic plans for growing old and feeble with a classic question: "Will you still need me, will you still feed me, when I'm 64?"

The recorded arrangement is suitably old-fashioned, with a music hall melody and a clarinet trio contrasting McCartney's youthful voice (he was 24 at the time).

Why pick 64?

When James Paul McCartney was born in 1942, the average life span of a British male was 63 years. His tongue-in-cheek prediction of what his golden years might be like was charming but way off the mark. Today at 76, he's healthy, vibrant, and the proud father of an 11-year-old daughter.

That's not exactly "wasting away" as he once described growing older.

When McCartney's song hit the airwaves in 1967, the Boomer's slogan was, "Never trust anyone over 30." Fueled by the hedonistic culture of the day, many of us thought people would be senile, comatose, or in a rest home by their 60's.

It's been 50 years since Sgt. Pepper taught the band to play, but McCartney's never slowed down. In 2005 (at age 63), he rocked the Super Bowl; his halftime show was viewed by 86 million people. Since turning 64, he's released over seven albums, a dozen singles, and numerous soundtracks.

In the process, this swinging senior has amassed a net worth of $1.2 billion.

Incidentally, McCartney wasn't alone on his "big six-four" milestone. Notables celebrating their 64th birthdays in 2006 included Harrison Ford, Aretha Franklin, Stephen Hawking, Martin Scorsese, Brian Wilson, Calvin Klein, Judge Judy Sheindlin, and Barbra Streisand.

Q. Twelve years later, how many of these 75-year-olds have retired?

A. If you said, "None of the above," you're right.

And that's the point. They're all working. Earning. Contributing to the greater good in their own ways.

In a *New York Times* article, Sam Roberts reported, "Americans live longer today…They also age more slowly, or so they say. Half the over-65 population define themselves as middle-aged or even young."

Roberts said that 64-year-olds today can expect to live an extra 16 years compared with folks born in 1942, and about four years longer than those who turned 64 when the famous song came out in 1967. He notes that writer Gail Sheehy says today's 64-year-olds have a "360-degree view of life." They may believe in yesterday, but they refuse to live there. "The new 64," Sheehy said, "is more like 84."

And that applies to entertainers, too—even those who naively predicted that life over 50 would not be worth living. In a 1975 interview, Mick Jagger sneered, "I'd rather be dead than singing 'Satisfaction' when I'm 45."

In case you're wondering, he's 75 now and still singing his classic hit. Turns out Jagger's shelf life was longer than sociologists could have predicted. This very rich grandpa is worth $360 million, with luxury abodes in London, Paris, Manhattan, and a private island.

Is *that* enough inspiration to keep rockin' past retirement age?

From 58-year-old Bono (worth $700M), to 71-year-old Jimmy Buffet (worth $450M), a growing army of active, creative second-halfers in *every* line of work—retail, manufacturing, technology, health care, sales, whatever—are breaking away from the old pattern of dropping back or existing in the shadows.

As 72-year-old Cher (worth $320M) sings, "The beat goes on."

I could list 100 more like her and there's no sign of any of them slowing down. Or losing their sense of humor. When Paul Simon turned 64, McCartney dialed him up and sang, "When I'm 64" over the phone.

In the 1970s, Clairol introduced a slogan for Loving Care that became an instant classic. The ad gurus on Madison Avenue assured millions of nervous women: "You're not getting older, you're getting better!"

That ad campaign sold truckloads of hair color kits, but it expressed an idea far bigger than covering up gray hair. It pinpointed a generation of Baby Boomers who were collectively turning (gasp!) 30 and were not excited about aging.

Today, being branded old at 29 sounds absurd, but Boomers grew up hearing the warning: "Don't trust anyone over 30." That shortsighted phrase was one of the most famous expressions of the turbulent '60s. It came out during the Free Speech Movement at UC Berkeley and grew to represent the entire generation gap. Incidentally, the student who coined the disparaging phrase—Jack Weinberg—is 78 years old.

In a similar vein, in 1965, The Who sang "My Generation." The guitar-smashing pop star who wrote the lyric, "I hope I die before I get old" was Pete Townshend. He's not dead. He's 73 and still doing concerts.

As for Sir Paul McCartney? He is entitled to a basic pension from the British government (about $156 a week) and a free transit pass to ride the subways, but the singer says he has no plans to retire.

Maybe he should redo his song as, "When I'm 94."

## LEAVE A LEGACY

As a young man, I was approached by Bernie Moray, CEO of Gorman's Furniture, headquartered in southeast Michigan. At that time, Gorman's had a successful retail operation, but was struggling with their office furniture division.

Under his proposal, Moray and I would each recapitalize the business with $100K. In turn, Bernie would give me 50 percent of the stock and I would run the business under his mentorship. When I stepped in, Gorman's Business Interiors (GBI) was losing $250K annually on $2.5M in sales. Over the next six years, we grew it to a high of $15M in sales with profits of approximately $250K.

During my eight years at Gorman's, I was blessed by my mentor's vast experience. Bernie Moray unselfishly shared his hard-earned wisdom.

Here is the amazing part—Bernie *still* owns Gorman's and provides active leadership at age 96. He obviously replaced retirement with intentional living.

Moray started in furniture back in 1949 and never lost his zeal. "I enjoy what I do and I do it well. The Lord has been good to me, and as long as I have the physical and mental capacity to work, I'll die in the saddle." When asked why he doesn't retire, he says, "Seeing my retired friends who are bored out of their skulls."

Here's an insight into how dynamic he is. Bernie played doubles tennis well into his 80's. In his 90's, one of his knees began giving him trouble. When he requested knee replacement surgery, doctors advised him to skip the procedure and simply slow down like a normal nonagenarian. But Bernie insisted, "I'm a busy guy. I've got a lot going on." Soon, he was back in action with a bionic knee and in the office every morning at seven o'clock sharp.

Don't you love that zest for life?

# Pushing Back on Old Age.

When President Franklin D. Roosevelt implemented Social Security in 1935, the average life expectancy in America was 61 years old. Today, it's 78.8 years (and increasing annually). The idea of retiring at age 65 is totally obsolete.

In a study called, "The Evolution of Adulthood," the late Dr. Elliott Jaques proposed a three-stage work model. He suggests that in light of new realities, our work life would be better understood if divided into "career thirds." Those thirds break down roughly as 18-40 (early adulthood), 40-62 (mid-adulthood), and my favorite, 62-85 (mature adulthood).

If that sounds odd, let me ask you this: are you more intelligent, qualified, and experienced at age 25, age 45, or age 65?

Of course, it's 65 by a mile!

Unless you're busting rocks for a living, you're at your most useful and valuable status in your *third* stage. And even if your job is manual labor, recent studies prove that senior citizens can enjoy a level of health and strength once thought impossible. Octogenarians and even nonagenarians can gain muscle mass, increase cardio efficiency, and improve flexibility with regular exercise. The same goes for mental capacity.

And recent breakthroughs in brain science show no drop-off in intelligence or learning ability either. With exercises that increase your brain cell's neuroplasticity, there's no reason we can't be sharp as a tack until we die.

Dr. Jaques asserts, "Old age has been pushed back by many years." He envisions a bright future for seniors. "A whole new stage of active life is open to them, with untold opportunities for continued intellectual growth and accomplishment."

The cultural stereotype of helpless, feeble, doddering seniors is false.

It's based on ignorance of nutrition, fitness, and the power of the human spirit.

Don't believe it?

A 103-year-old golfer named Gus Andreone hit a hole-in-one at Sarasota's Palm Aire Country Club in 2014. He's done it *eight* times and looks forward to doing it again. Elsie McLean aced her hole-in-one in 2007 at the young age of 102.

———

"It's never too late to do something amazing," says Daniel Wald-schmidt. His book, *Edgy Conversations: How Ordinary People Can Achieve Outrageous Success* chronicles accomplishments by older folks. Their exploits might inspire you to call off that retirement party:

- At 75, Cornelius Vanderbilt began buying railroads.

- At 75, cancer survivor Barbara Hillary reached the North Pole.

- At 76, Nelson Mandela was inaugurated president of South Africa.

- At 77, John Glenn became the oldest person to go into space.

So many startling achievements occur in our second half. But why slow down *ever*? The goals hit by folks over 80 are even more illuminating:

- At 85, Theodor Mommsen received a Nobel Prize in Literature.

- At 86, Tony Bennett sang in front of 100,000 fans at the World Series.

- Retired Lt. Col. James Warren was a navigator in the Tuskegee Airmen. At 87, he became the oldest person in the world to receive a pilot's license.

- At 88, Michelangelo designed the Church of Santa Maria degli Angeli.

- At 89, Arthur Rubinstein performed a sold-out recital in Carnegie Hall.

And the "super seniors" (those above 90) are blazing new trails every day:

- At 92, Paul Spangler finished his fourteenth full marathon.

- At 93, P.G. Wodehouse wrote his 97 novel and was knighted.

- Betty White is almost older than sliced bread. No, that's not a put down. It's a fact. Betty was born in 1922. The bread slicer was invented in 1920. At age 96, White's still active, still productive, and the poster girl for a new wave of senior citizens who aren't going away anytime soon.

Dr. Leila Denmark was an American pediatrician who actively practiced medicine until the age of 103. This super-centenarian lived to be 114.

# Myth Busters.

One persistent myth drives me up the wall. It's the common belief that "Life past 80 or 90 is not worth living." People falsely believe the quality of life in our advanced years will automatically be vastly inferior. They're afraid an extended life span simply means more years of declining health and limited functionality.

I can bust that myth with hard facts and countless examples of seniors who can outrun, out-ski, out-dance, out-sing, and outswim folks half their age.

People tell me they don't *want* to reach 100 because they'll be broken down and frail. In that case, I wouldn't want to either! But that's not what medicine is predicting for future centenarians. In fact, many say there are *no* physiological reasons why we can't be fit, firm, and fully cognizant for our entire life.

According to British researcher, Dr. Aubrey De Grey, growing old may soon be obsolete. Dr. De Grey claims, "We have a 50/50 chance of bringing aging under a decisive level of medical control within the next 25 years."

A biomedical gerontologist, Dr. De Grey claims there's a child alive right now who will live to be 150—something Ray Kurzweil predicted decades ago. Of course, not everyone agrees, but Dr. De Grey feels that within his own lifetime, doctors will have all the tools they need to "cure" aging.

This doctor—and he's not alone in this—describes aging as the lifelong accumulation of molecular and cellular damage throughout the body. He sees a time when people will go to doctors for regular "maintenance," including gene therapies, stem cell therapies, immune stimulation, and other advanced medical techniques to keep us from aging.

And it's coming our way at exponential speed.

Two of the leaders in the field are Craig Venter, Ph.D., and Peter Diamandis, M.D, cofounders of Human Longevity, Inc. The company's stated goal is to "extend and enhance the healthy high-performance life span and change the face of aging." They're doing that via intensive research in human genomics, DNA sequencing, and synthetic biology. (Check out the latest advances at *humanlongevity.com*.) But not everyone is thrilled about it. To some, the promise of longer life conjures up hospitals and hospices stuffed with old people demanding care and consuming resources—draining coffers already hard-pressed to pay for the elderly.

Science says that kind of linear pessimism is sadly out of date. "This is absolutely not a matter of keeping people alive in a bad state of health," says Dr. De Grey. "This is about preventing people from getting sick as a result of old age."

Dr. Venter agrees, "Aging is the single biggest risk factor for virtually every significant human disease." Cure aging and the rest is easy.

Think about it—our later years don't have to be a train wreck or a hardship.

That might just be the best news you'll ever read. As medical science grows exponentially, breakthroughs in preventative geriatrics will deliver long life as a *side effect* of delivering better health.

Dr. Diamandis has a passion for extending the healthy human life span. Recently, on his website, *Singularity Hub*, he discussed some remarkably good news for our generation with futurist Dr. Ray Kurzweil. Kurzweil has a revolutionary concept he calls "longevity escape velocity"—the inflection point at which, for every year that you're alive, science will be able to extend your life for more than a year.

This tipping point in medical science is nicknamed the "breakout," and Kurzweil says the reversal of traditional aging trends will take place soon. "I predict it's likely just another 10 to 12 years before the general public will hit longevity escape velocity. At that point, biotechnology is going to have taken over medicine."

I urge you to use that optimistic prediction as an incentive to do all you can *now* to make sure you'll be around when it occurs. Kurzweil adds, "The next decade is going to be a profound revolution."

Dr. Diamandis explains why the next decade is so pivotal. "Scientists are continually extending the human life span, helping us cure heart disease, cancer, and eventually, neurodegenerative disease. This will keep accelerating as technology improves."

Sound like science fiction? It's real, and it's coming. So our job now is to stay alive until it gets here. That includes exercise, diet, and safe driving. Dr. Kurzweil jokes, "Wear your seat belt until we get the self-driving cars going."

Of course, you might want to rely on your good genes, like Nathan Birnbaum.

Sorry. You might know him better as George Burns. At age 79, Burns experienced a revival in his career and won an Oscar for Best Supporting Actor in the 1975 smash, *The Sunshine Boys*. He started in vaudeville in 1903 and was a star in radio, films, and television. He did live stand-up comedy into his 90's and smoked four cigars a day (he estimated smoking a total of 300,000 stogies).

Despite the health risks posed by his trademark cigars, George Burns continued happily working until he died at age 100.

## LEAVE A LEGACY

How about the other side of the health equation?
Dr. Shigeaki Hinohara started practicing medicine back in 1941. For 76 years, Dr. Hinohara made daily rounds at St. Luke's hospital in Tokyo. "I put in 18 hours, seven days a week and love every minute." Still active and working, he passed away in 2017 at age 105. Besides his medical and teaching duties, Dr. Hinohara had published 150 books since his 75 birthday. His simple advice for a long, happy life was to *stay thin, stay busy*, and *never retire*.
But his biggest single tip was to *help others*. "In our later years, we should strive to contribute to society. Since age 65, I have worked as a volunteer."

# Getting Older and Better.

For decades, Baby Boomers were the largest generation in US history.

Not anymore.

In April 2016, the Pew Research Center announced that Millennials passed Baby Boomers as America's biggest generation. This shift is due to the influx of young immigrants and is based on population estimates released by the US Census Bureau. If you're counting, Millennials (ages 18 to 34) now number 75.4 million, surpassing the 74.9 million Baby Boomers (ages 51 to 69). And Generation X (ages 35 to 50) is also on track to pass the Boomers by 2028.

Boomers may not be the *largest* group anymore, but they still hold the purse strings. That's according to a McKinsey Global Institute report released in 2016. Roughly two-thirds of new car sales are to folks over 50. And half of all Harley-Davidson buyers are 50 and up. Same for categories like home improvement. Verne Harnish says the days of advertising gurus catering to youth are fading out. The real buying power lies with the 60-plus group. How much power? Two-thirds of GDP growth in the US and Western Europe will come from older adults.

And they're still the 800-pound gorilla in the job market.

Numbers indicate that Boomers control approximately 80 percent of America's aggregate net worth. And they're predicted to spend more to maintain their active lifestyles than any previous generation.

Which makes us a force to be reckoned with, not retired.

"Boomers are the largest demographic force we have, in terms of volume, wealth, consumer spending, and jobs," according to Chris Hyzy, chief investment officer at US Trust. He's quoted in a Merrill Lynch study called "The End of Old."

The same article quotes Joe Coughlin, director of the prestigious MIT AgeLab. "Previous generations were expected to age politely and cope with the aches and pains that defined retirement. Boomers are saying, 'I will not just live longer, I will live better!'"

That could be our mantra: *Not just longer, better.*

# Moving Forward or Slipping Backward?

"Old age and treachery will always beat youth and exuberance."

That was Paul Newman's motto. And the Oscar-winning actor wasn't kidding. At the age of 70, he became the oldest driver to win a major auto race, capturing the 24 Hours of Daytona in 1995. At 79, he raced in the rigorous off-road Baja 1000. At 80, he competed again at Daytona.

Newman lived with gusto, and instead of retiring, he started a line of food products called Newman's Own—with all profits going to charity. As of today, his hobby has donated over $460 million.

But were Newman's latter-day successes a rarity? Or can any one of us shine our brightest in our second half?

Absolutely yes. Untold numbers of innovators—from artists like Monet and Cézanne, to writers like Robert Frost and Dr. Seuss—often produce their life's greatest work well *after* middle age.

Frank Lloyd Wright was perhaps our greatest architect. His most recognized masterpiece is the Guggenheim Museum in New York. He designed the unique spiral structure in the *last fifteen years* of his life, perfecting it up until his death at age 91.

That eye-opener is important for two reasons:

1. **Our group is living longer.** An American born today has a projected life span that's over 20 years longer than a baby born in 1925.

2. **Our group is expanding.** Each year between now and 2030, another 3,560,000 Americans turn 65—that's larger than the population of 25 of our 50 states.

This intelligent, creative people group must not be allowed to vegetate, hibernate, or otherwise waste their time and talent.

Fortunately, when it comes to creativity, experts concur that age really *is* only a number. More and more, we see that *experience*—in life, in relationships, in business—is necessary to produce work of value that stands the test of time.

We cannot be static. We're either moving forward or we're slipping backwards.

There's no treading water in this Exponential Age. Like my friend and mentor, Dan Sullivan (creator of The Strategic Coach Program) says, "Always make your future bigger than your past."

I'm a living, breathing example of that advice. And this book is proof. I'd have never published anything on this scale prior to age sixty. But the fact that you're holding this book is evidence that we can always trend upward.

Here's my point: You can go the way society is telling you—pull over and move to the curb. Or you can choose the express lane I suggest—pursuing abundance and exponential growth in the second half of life.

———

Some of you have ample funds to glide through your senior years in leisure. I suggest you become active in a nonprofit or consult pro bono in a field you're experienced in. For everyone else, I advocate you keep working. Today, a higher percentage of retirement-age Americans are working than any time since 1900.

And that's a good thing. These industrious folks are earning paychecks—supporting themselves *and* contributing to the global economy.

But earning money is only the beginning. Staying mentally and physically active in the workforce is literally keeping them younger, sharper, happier, and more engaged with the world. They're living a longer, fuller, richer, and more purposeful life by helping themselves and society.

*Who wouldn't want that?*

Sadly, not everybody.

A healthy 75-year-old with no serious medical issues ended her life at a suicide clinic in Switzerland simply because she "didn't want to grow old." The British woman said she wasn't depressed or incapacitated but had once had shingles and was annoyed by tinnitus (ringing in the ears). Hardly what I'd call a terminal illness.

When asked why she chose to die, the woman said she wanted her adult children to enjoy their lives without having to care for her. She blogged that she would not put that "burden" on her kids.

Apparently, she saw old age as a *burden* instead of a *blessing*. She saw her golden years as a nonproductive life stage—years of useless hobbling about without the possibility of making a positive contribution to the world.

Overwhelming evidence contradicts that worn-out thinking. At age 82, director Woody Allen just keeps the movies coming. As of now, he has written and directed over 52 films, with no end in sight. During an interview for *The Wall Street Journal*, Don Steinberg asked Allen if he would make a final "closing statement" type of movie someday.

Allen replied, "I just work year after year, and so far, it seems that I'm in good health. I feel energetic. My dad lived to slightly over 100. My mother lived to almost 100. My guess is I'll just keep working as long as people keep backing me. I have a lot of stories I'd like to tell."

Allen keeps a drawer stuffed with notes for future movies. To relax (and stay mentally sharp) he plays jazz clarinet at New York's Carlyle Hotel on Monday nights. Seats near the stage will cost you $245 a pop. Instead of writing a final swan song and quitting, Allen says, "I see myself dying in the saddle."

*Dying in the saddle.* How much better is that attitude than taking poison because you don't want to be a burden? (Incidentally, over 1,000 folks have paid $5,000 each for an assisted suicide in Zurich.)

Speaking of saddles, we can't forget the actor who debuted as Rowdy Yates on *Rawhide* back in 1959. Since then, Clint Eastwood's been in over 50 feature films as actor, director, producer, or composer. At 88, he's Hollywood's oldest working director, and he's not slowing down.

Eastwood told AP film writer, Jake Coyle, "You have more experience as you get older...more to draw on. You can experiment with things. You can be 21 or 81...If you tell yourself, 'I'm too old to do that'—bullshit. You're not too old to do anything."

The Oscar winner once known as Dirty Harry refuses to quit. "I always work hard to keep sharp. I think it's very important, as one ages, to learn new things. That's why I have no ambition to retire."

As we've seen, Woody and Eastwood are not alone in their zest for living.

Famed violinist, Isaac Stern, titled his autobiography, *My First 79 Years*. Stern performed brilliantly onstage until his death at 81. In his later years, he taught master classes and led the drive to save historic Carnegie Hall from demolition.

That's intentional living!

That's what I'm shooting for. Plus a few more years for good luck.

# More Inventive Than Ever.

What do Mother Teresa, Alexander Graham Bell, and Mary Kay all have in common?

They were all brilliantly productive well into old age.

Many people we admire made their *biggest* contributions late in life. People like Julia Child, Paul Cezanne, and Harry Potter's creator, J. K. Rowling, all defied stereotypes and flourished as late bloomers.

As recently as 75 years ago, the elderly were honored, respected, and consulted. Being older was a sign of wisdom and authority, not frailty and irrelevance. Their place in the home was often to help raise the grandkids and transfer essential values while parents worked. Think of *The Waltons*—three generations living under one roof and everyone benefiting. This fictional Depression-era family was able to endure hardships because of the traditions and nurturing provided by the grandparents. It wasn't until the modern era of fragmented families and consumerism that society began pushing older folks aside.

I say *enough* of that.

Washington's generation founded our nation. Lincoln's generation preserved the Union. Our parents' generation saved democracy. And now our generation has a similar responsibility to the *next* generation—a role that does not end at age 55 or 65 or even 85. No coach tells his star players they can quit playing at halftime, head for the locker room, and watch the rest of the game on TV.

# What Can the Older Offer the Younger?

The majority of new entrepreneurs are over 50. According to the Kauffman Foundation, the age group starting the greatest number of new businesses is 55 to 64.

I know. It's hard to believe. I can hear it now: "Doesn't the future belong to kids like Mark Zuckerberg who cranked up Facebook in college?"

Not necessarily, says Vivek Wadhwa. He's vice president of innovation and research at Singularity University, and he pushes back in a PBS blog titled, "The Truth About Entrepreneurs: Twice as Many Over 50 Than Under 25."

## LEAVE A LEGACY

Sometimes the health that is improved is not your own.
Sam Teitelbaum is the 74-year-old owner of Montreal-based AllerAir. Yet, he became a manufacturer quite late in life. He worked in his family's clothing store for 25 years. His wife had severe allergies, though, and her suffering led him to study air purifiers. When she was diagnosed with multiple chemical sensitivity (MCS), Teitelbaum set out to develop an air purifier that would not only remove particles, but airborne chemicals and odors. He researched and then created a new carbon-based air-cleaning technology. This initiative quickly established AllerAir as unique in the industry. Today, his company manufactures residential and commercial air-purification systems—with over 100 different models.

> The company earns $5 million annually, having seen 20 percent growth every year for the past 12 years.

Wadhwa says, "Myths abound about the young entrepreneurs who dreamed up crazy ideas while in their dorm room, raised millions of dollars in venture capital, and started billion-dollar businesses. But these are just the outliers. The typical entrepreneur is…a middle-aged professional who learns about a market need and starts a company with his own savings."

That's because we've got hard-won, battle-tested skills in entrepreneurship. Skills that can transform our economy and create millions of new jobs.

That applies to advances in cutting-edge technology, too. Wadhwa wrote in *The Washington Post*: "The claim that only the young can effect change has been disproved not only by Apple, but also by founders, inventors, and executives at almost every major technology company, including Google, LinkedIn, and Intel. Qualcomm, for example, was founded by Irwin Jacobs when he was 52 and Andrew Viterbi, who was 50."

He adds, "Steve Jobs was 52 when he announced the iPhone. That was in 2007. Years later, the Apple cofounder introduced the MacBook Air, App Store and iPad. Tim Cook, who was 51 when he took over from Jobs, is building on his legacy. They both shattered a myth that the young rule the technology industry."

Most of the big fish in the real-life *Shark Tank* are second-halfers. Sure, the media loves to spotlight youngsters like the (then)

17-year-old Nick D'Aloisio. This high schooler sold his news-reading app to Yahoo for close to $30 million. That's cool. That's exponential technology. But the nitty-gritty fact is the majority of new business start-ups today are coming from the over-50 crowd.

Writing in *Business Insider*, Sarah Schmalbruch agrees that retirement often conjures up the image of an elderly couple sitting in Florida reading the paper. But it turns out many adults are challenging the traditional definition of aging.

Schmalbruch reports the highest rate of entrepreneurial activity in the last 10 years has been in the 55 to 64 age bracket. And more than one in three new businesses are started by an entrepreneur over 50.

That's not to say that this is a new phenomenon. After all, the founders of McDonald's, Coca-Cola, and even the inventor of the Taser were over 50 when they launched their businesses.

Ray Kroc was driving around the country selling milkshake machines when a tiny hamburger joint in California ordered eight of his units. Curious, Kroc decided to pay them a visit. Impressed with the operation, he convinced Dick and Mac McDonald to franchise their drive-in restaurant in San Bernardino. Kroc eventually purchased the company at age 52.

How'd that work out for an over-the-hill middle-aged guy?

Glad you asked. McDonald's stopped posting hamburger sales when they topped $99 billion in 1993. Today, they earn roughly $28 billion a year.

Not bad for a late-bloomer.

Speaking of fast food, don't forget Colonel Harland Sanders—he founded Kentucky Fried Chicken at age 65.

———

Seasoned businesspeople obviously have the chops to revolutionize and energize the American economy though entrepreneurship. And when it comes to *inventions*, older is definitely better.

"There's a boom in inventions by people over 50," said John Calvert, director of the United Inventors Association. In a *New York Times* article by Constance Gustke, Calvert says over 60 percent of the Association's members are older Americans.

Gustke's article, "More Adults Are Becoming Inventors," heralds the explosion in innovations being brought to market by seniors. It backs my theory that your best and brightest output is yet to come.

Business author, Michael Hyatt, agrees. "If you feel like you're getting passed up by brilliant kids with bright ideas, you're not. Your best years are either now or just coming. Set big goals. And stay with it."

If you're north of 50, take heart—you've got an unfair advantage! As Hyatt says, "Age isn't a disqualifier for entrepreneurs. It's more like a prerequisite."

# Is There Really an Upside to Aging?

Research has shown that older people have increased empathy, enhanced creativity, and the ability to better communicate on emotional levels.

*Times* writer, Constance Gustke, also quotes Dr. Gary Small, professor of psychiatry and director of the UCLA Longevity Center. Dr. Small says aging has its advantages. "Everyone thinks that aging is a negative process. But that's not necessarily the case. An aging brain can see patterns better."

Dr. Small says short-term memory may decline, but people become more empathetic as they get older. "And this is an essential ingredient in creating products for others," he adds, "so you can see what an audience needs."

At 87, James West is living proof. West obtained 11 patents when he was over 60 and invented a microphone that doesn't need a power supply. "Anyone can be equally inventive at 75 as at 40," said West.

Did you catch that? *Equally inventive.* That's good news for a country being blessed with a bumper crop of 420 people turning 65 every hour.

Speaking of inventors, if you're reading this by electric light, you can thank Thomas Edison. Biographers calculate he averaged one patent every two weeks during his entire adult life. Young or old, he never stopped contributing to society, and his tireless mind never stopped working.

Neither will yours—if you keep using your creativity, regardless of age.

A "bubbling imagination" is all you need, said Warren Tuttle, president of the United Inventors Association. "Some inventors drop out of high school," he said, "and some are Ph.D.'s." He claims that older inventors can better focus on a project and have more "stick-to-itiveness" than younger workers.

Still not convinced? Ben Franklin was 76 when he invented bifocals.

*"Age doesn't matter. An open mind does."*

—TIM FERRISS

# CREATING YOUR LEGACY MAP

## HOW TO ENVISION AND PLAN THE BEST POSSIBLE FUTURE FOR THE BEST POSSIBLE YOU.

*"My goal is to build a life I don't need a vacation from."*

—ROB HILL SR.

*"The tragedy in life doesn't lie in not reaching your goal. It lies in having no goal to reach."*

—BENJAMIN E. MAYS

# More Than a Bucket List.

May I take a quick shot at profiling you?

My guess is you're successful, well-educated, and highly motivated.

But something inside you keeps asking, *Is that all there is? Have I collected all this experience and skill just for myself? Is that really the goal?*

If these questions haunt you even a little, then you and I are alike.

We're a different breed. Which is why we need a different route to a different future. That's why I created the Legacy Map.

With this tool, you can best position yourself to capitalize on the opportunities of the Exponential Age. At first, the process seems simple, even linear. But with continuous use, the Legacy Map will follow the exponential curve to what I've dubbed the "Exponential Catalyst"—the point where the curve takes a pronounced shift upward.

The Map is not about wishful thinking or bucket lists. It's about this hot furnace burning inside us that's full of ideas and churning with what is possible.

A risk worth taking.

As we hit milestone birthdays, it's easy to accept a life with fewer options and less adventure. Let me ask you, *Is your world shrinking or expanding?*

My dad had been the CEO of a worldwide corporation, but within six years of retirement, he was a shell of his former self. His life had shrunk to a sofa, a cocktail, and the daily newspaper. When I'd ask how he was doing, he'd reply, "I'm surviving." That answer drove me up the wall. He eventually perked up, but without meaningful work or a worthy cause to keep him active and alert, his retirement years were a shadow of his former contribution.

I vowed to never follow that pattern. I wrestled with questions: *What is it that constricts our worldview in the second half of life? Why do we feel the panicky urge to control our environment? Are there psychological or physiological factors that I need to overcome so I don't grind to a halt?*

Around age 50, I sensed my own world beginning to shrink.

I was going out less, meeting fewer people, and turning down social events. I was shifting from extrovert to introvert. I resolved to counteract this trend by deliberately injecting a degree of risk into my life. In the 2016 movie, *Papa*, Ernest Hemingway's character chides a nervous young writer, "The only value we have as human beings are the risks we're willing to take."

There's truth in that. Call it courage, spunk, nerve, whatever; taking risks is like using a muscle. Activity makes it grow, neglect makes it atrophy. That's why I still ski the expert-level runs (even though they're scarier each year). Same for my cross-country snowmobiling expeditions. Last year, I rode from Ontario to eastern Quebec— 3,000 miles in 14 days.

Yes, I might fall off. Yes, I might break something. But if I don't push out of my comfort zone—on a regular basis—my universe will close in until I'm no longer enjoying the unlimited options out there.

So I push the boundaries. Within reason.

For example, I know adults who jump out of planes. In fact, President George H.W. Bush celebrated his 90th birthday by making a tandem parachute jump. I respect that. But skydiving's not my thing. Taking appropriate risks will look different for each of us. We don't need to be unwise or foolish just to prove something. On the other hand, we should *never* be afraid to learn a new skill or stick our necks out for what we believe. We should *never* be afraid to take our life's passion and exercise it in new ways that benefit others.

Anyone ready for a new blueprint can create a Legacy Map. Anyone who is entrepreneurial in their thinking. Anyone who knows that the upside of achieving success is not playing endless rounds of golf, but in continuously creating a future of their own choosing. Anyone who believes they have special gifts, uncommon awareness, and a unique purpose.

Most of all, anyone with an outlook that's expanding, not shrinking.

If that sounds like you, get ready to ask yourself the dangerous question, "What is my unique contribution to this world?"

## A New Map for a New You.

"We need a new map of life."

That was Marc Freedman in a *USA TODAY* article by Kerry Hannon, called, "Tips on Navigating the New Midlife Stage." Freedman founded the nonprofit Encore and, like me, is an outspoken critic of traditional retirement.

Freedman says that in the past, "The 50s and 60s meant retirement, grandparenthood, senior discounts and early-bird specials." But with longer, healthier life spans, that's all changing. He calls this new season of life "the Encore Stage." I define this stage as work that combines continued income with greater personal meaning—and your best chance to make an impact.

Freedman's book, *Encore: Finding Work That Matters in the Second Half of Life*, insists that Baby Boomers want second-half work that offers purpose and gives meaning to life. And statistics show they're stepping up in record numbers.

"The surge of people into this new stage of life is one of the most important social phenomena of the new century." Freedman says, "Never before have so many people had so much experience and the time and the capacity to do something significant with it."

In a report commissioned by Encore and MetLife, Freedman posed the question, "What if, over time, 100,000 people…were persuaded to launch 10-year encore careers? That would mean one million years of service dedicated to areas like education, poverty, and the environment."

Like me, he sees Boomers as a catalytic mechanism for change. "Applying this human talent and experience to the big challenges of our time could be as profound a contribution as those made possible by new technologies or even massive infusions of philanthropic dollars."

Tapping into that talent pool is what the Legacy Map is all about.

# What Needs to Change?

*Someday, I'll take that trip. Someday, I'll write that book. Someday, I'll get in shape...or change jobs...or patch up that broken relationship.*

Trouble is, someday never comes. At least not by wishful thinking.

Hitting your "someday goals" takes effort. And it takes a plan. A *written* plan that can turn someday into reality.

By using a Legacy Map, you can identify and neutralize the barriers between you and the life you've always wanted. Being intentional and fastidious about aligning your life around what matters most is key to the mapping process.

Over years of coaching, I've observed two patterns:

- First, we all have goals. You could probably jot down a dozen. Beyond the obvious clichés (fame, fortune, romance, etc.), we all want a better, more fulfilling future. In our hearts, we long to be unshackled—to live without fear or pretense, to dump the excuses for never reaching our full potential.

- Second, most of us already have a rough idea about what we should add or subtract in our lives to reach those goals. In some corner of our brain, we *know* what needs to be done to spend less, save more, lose weight, whatever.

So why do we get lost in the weeds?

In *Alice in Wonderland*, a confused Alice asks the Cheshire Cat for directions. He replies, "If you don't know where you're going, any road will get you there."

Without a clear destination and an accurate map, we'll never know if we're on the right path. Behavioral expert, James Clear, says, "If you commit to nothing, you'll be distracted by everything."

In Section 1, we talked about the unnerving speed and scale of change in the Exponential Age. To navigate in this accelerated and unpredictable landscape, we need new thinking. Time-tested models won't cut it. In my opinion, up to 80 percent of today's knowledge may be irrelevant in 10 years. The Legacy Map is a goal-setting tool, but beyond that it's a process that: (1) develops exponential thinking; and (2) helps you chart a course according to exponential markers.

## Why a Legacy Map?

Life is not a theoretical or intellectual exercise. It's real. And as Ferris Bueller warned, it "moves pretty fast."

The Legacy Map allows us to keep up—*and* to chart our own course. Over time, continued use of the Map helps retrain our brain from the old linear *modus operandi* to fresh thinking. Remember, there are only two choices. We can be a disrupter or be disrupted by the tides of change washing over us.

Of course, nobody can see perfectly into the future. So the Map allows for adjustments along the way. Changing direction is not failure; it's learning as we go and seeing mistakes as opportunities for growth. As author Rick Warren says, we're products of our past, but not prisoners of it.

Like any map, the Legacy Map is a set of directions. What's unique about it is the "character guideposts" along the journey. It's not just where we go, but how we get there that matters. Determining our values—and sticking to them—shapes us into the high-integrity people we want our kids and grandkids to emulate. (I explore the importance of character in Section 7.)

As you can guess, the Legacy Map is not a "survival guide" to growing old gracefully. Nor is it a guide to creating a financially stable cocoon of leisure. Quite the opposite! Plenty of authors and speakers are telling you how to invest your *money*. I'm telling you how to invest your *years*—with the highest possible returns on your work experience and entrepreneurial knowledge.

My desire for liberty, abundance, and ultimately for legacy compels me to share what I've learned. I've devoted my life to helping others swim against the cultural tide. If you jump in, I'll show you a path to freedom, meaning, and impact.

# Living Your Legacy Requires Two Commitments.

I've been a goal setter for over 30 years and have learned much about what does and doesn't work. I've learned a lot from trial and error. But I've learned even more by standing on the shoulders of those who mentored me directly or indirectly through books on how to be intentional about *living your legacy*.

After years of coaching people through the journey, I have boiled the process down to just two commitments—"Be Inspired" and "Manage Your Energy."

1. The first, *being inspired*, comes from seeing in your mind a bigger future than you have today, thus always making your future bigger than your past. In the next few pages, I will give you three powerful processes to clarify an inspirational future that is compelling to pursue.

2. The second, *managing your energy*, is where the rubber hits the road and where you turn your vision into reality. In order to make progress towards that inspiring future you created, you must take the first step and start today!

The process is illustrated in the simple graphic below. This is the framework to follow in completing your Legacy Map:

Be Inspired

- **See Your Future** (Visual)
- **Write Your Story** (Emotional)
- **Set Your Goals** (Measurable)

Manage Your Energy

- **Practice Your Habits** (Actionable)
- **Be Responsible** (Accountable)

# BE INSPIRED

## See Your Future: *Visual*

Imagine yourself training for the pole vault at age 95.

That's what Olga Kotelko was doing when she died in 2014. After winning over 100 gold medals in a dozen senior track and field events, Kotelko refused to picture herself languishing in a rocking chair. Instead, she had a vision of sailing up in the air and over a crossbar. She saw herself standing on the winner's podium in front of her great-grandchildren!

This remarkable athlete refused to slow down. Instead of resting on her laurels, Kotelko was visioning herself taking on yet another unlikely feat of strength and agility. Her life and legacy reinforce what I've said over and over—*how we think* and *what we believe about ourselves* have a direct impact on how we experience everything, not just emotionally but physically.

Walt Disney believed in the power of visioning. A few years ago, on a trip to Walt Disney World in Orlando, I toured an exhibit of his office and studio. His walls were literally covered from floor to ceiling with sketches, drawings, and plans for the future Disney World and Epcot Center. He surrounded himself with his *vision* long before he created its *reality.*

Disney famously said, "If you can dream it, you can do it. Always remember that this whole thing was started with a dream and a mouse."

According to *MarketWatch.com*, that dream now has a market cap of $173 billion.

Disney started his company in 1923 and built it slowly in a *linear* way. Then, in 1962, he expanded his vision *exponentially* by launching a team of dreamers—a group combining unbridled imagination with innovative engineering. He called their creative process "imagineering." Today these "imagineers" are still the driving force behind the Disney brand's iconic attractions and visitor experiences. Their motto is, "We make the magic." For them, visioning is "blue sky speculation"—dreaming with zero limitations and a goal of "the boldest, wildest, best ideas."

I mention Disney's dream team to inspire *you*.

Don't hold back. Don't skimp. Don't envision a wimpy future.

Business trainer, Brian Tracy says, "All successful people are big dreamers. They imagine what their future could be, ideal in every respect, and then they work every day toward their distant vision, goal, or purpose."

Visioning a healthy and productive future will literally change your worldview and ultimately your life. To repeat my metaphor, visioning (both in written and visual form) is like reprogramming a computer. Be aware that your old data (hurts, habits, epic fails, etc.) are lurking below the surface and could resurface if triggered. You can disarm the triggers by overwriting those neural pathways and connections with new "software" (your vision board).

As someone said, we aren't limited by our abilities, but by our vision.

Of course, it's not only the size or audacity of the goals that count. It's your perseverance and determination to *reach* those goals that carry the day. Since it's going to require significant effort, make sure your vision lines up with the core values you will truly and passionately hold onto at all costs.

In the *Harvard Business Review*, Jim Collins addressed this, "A well-conceived vision consists of two major components: *core ideology* and *envisioned future.*"

Collins adds, "Core ideology defines what we stand for and why we exist. The envisioned future is what we aspire to become, to achieve, to create—something that will require significant change and progress to attain."

## The Power of Pull.

> *"If you're working on something you really care about, you don't have to be pushed. The vision pulls you."*

That was Steve Jobs. He knew the power of a vision. So did people like Winston Churchill, Mahatma Gandhi, and Nelson Mandela. Throughout time, vision has moved leaders, technologies, and entire nations with unstoppable force.

In my own life, I've found that creating a compelling physical vision of my future is an incredibly powerful motivator and catalytic mechanism.

I've completed several vision boards throughout my life. In the beginning, I cut out pictures from magazines and populated a board with motivating images and statements. Even in its simplest form, I found the exercise beneficial. That's why I've repeated it and experimented with formats—from hand-painted boards to digital versions that anyone can create with a click.

Scientists say our minds have two primary gateways for things like dreaming, imagining, and visualizing. One is *language*; the other is *pictures*. In creating your personal vision board, I suggest using both. You can use stock photos or your personal photographs and favorite images. Likewise, you can use motivational quotes or insert your own text and stories.

Finding the right combination of motivating words and inspiring pictures will convey the vision of your future that most stimulates your imagination.

Using web-based tools at *VizBe.com*, you can quickly develop your own unique vision board. Choose to create a screensaver or print out a color poster—whatever visual reminder motivates you best. Your strategic combination of text and images will be a constant incentive to pursue your passion.

In my case, I went a step further and paid a graphic artist to draw my personal journey on a four-foot board. (It's mounted prominently in my office.) Regardless of format, it's important we meditate on our vision board frequently.

Why display it? Why not stuff it in a closet?

Because our *subconscious* mind is so powerful.

For better or worse, our brain works round the clock, trying to actualize whatever positive or negative statements we feed it. By physically seeing our future plotted on a vision board, our subconscious begins to attract opportunities and people to help fulfill that vision.

## LEAVE A LEGACY

Visioning works! Three years ago, I was introduced to a young visionary and entrepreneur named Natalia Petraszczuk. An early adapter to the concept of visioning, Petraszczuk was influenced by the phenomenally successful launch of a book and video titled, *The Secret* by Rhonda Byrne. Endorsed by Oprah, Byrne's bestseller gave examples of how the power of visioning and intentionality had influenced her life, as well as people throughout history. She encouraged her readers to use the age-old techniques. Petraszczuk quickly picked up that it is not enough to simply have a positive mental attitude. She intuitively realized that one of the best routes to achieving your goals is visualizing positive, focused, specific outcomes—and putting them on a customized vision board.

Excited to share the process, Petraszczuk looked for ways to streamline and simplify the creation of effective vision boards—by experimenting with analog formats (cutting pictures out of magazines) and upgrading to digital (creating electronic vision boards utilizing stock images, motivational phrases, and inspiring quotes). Today, her vision has been realized, and you are able to access the tool at *VizBe.com*. By using it, you can easily create your own electronic vision board and tie that vision to measurable goals.

Science and medicine are starting to agree. Dr. Aviva Romm, a Yale–trained M.D. says, "The process of creating a vision board... allows for the suspension of your thinking mind and the surfacing of subconscious hopes, dreams, and desires. It allows you to get in touch with you—uncensored—and to take what you discover and make it manifest in a creative, pictorial mind map."

Does it work? Dr. Romm says, "When we make our dreams concrete by turning them into achievable goals and putting these onto paper, whether in writing or through artistic expression, we are more likely to realize them."

She adds, "It's amazing what can happen when we send our intentions out there…creating intention and making it manifest visually, can be an important proactive and nourishing tool for making shifts happen in your life."

From personal experience, I can tell you it works. Be sure to visit your vision board daily (even just a few moments) and experience your future on an emotional level—feel yourself in your envisioned future. Keeping the vision alive and in front of your nose will help it come to pass.

(See the Appendix for the graphic of John's Vision Board.)

# BE INSPIRED

## Write Your Story: *Emotional*

How important is writing down your vision?

English business magnate Richard Branson says, "Write down every single idea you have, no matter how big or small."

The Hebrew writer of *Habakkuk* agrees: "Write the vision and make it plain."

So, write your vision down in as much detail as possible. Napoleon Hill urged picking *specific* dates and dollar amounts when creating a goal or vision.

Can the power of the pen be proven? A study at Dominican University by psychology professor Gail Matthews recently confirmed the boost in results that comes by committing our goals to paper. Dr. Matthews conducted a clinical study on nearly 300 participants attempting to reach various goals. She discovered people are 33 percent more likely to achieve their stated goals just by *writing them down* and *sharing them with a friend*.

To which I would add, the more specific you are, the better.

In his book, *A Lapsed Anarchist's Approach to Building a Great Business,* Ari Weinzweig wrote a highly detailed vision of his company at a *future* point in time—describing how it will impact employees, stakeholders, and surrounding communities in the year 2020. (Weinzweig is cofounder of Zingerman's—an Ann Arbor, Michigan, business that *Inc.* magazine named "The coolest small company in America.") Inspired by Weinzweig's example, my written vision of the future has a specific date and is anchored by a specific financial net worth goal.

I included details of how I will reach that financial target, along with what catalytic events and people will be involved. Like Weinzweig, I wrote down the impact that reaching my goal will make, and what I intend to do with the achieved success and resulting profits (mostly philanthropic).

I've modified it slightly with insights and improvements over the years. And I continue to tweak it. But it's basically intact. John Maxwell said, "Visions don't change, they are only refined. Plans rarely stay the same and are scrapped or adjusted as needed. Be stubborn about the vision, but flexible with your plan."

As part of my morning ritual, I will at times re-read this vision daily and/or modify it slightly to reflect where my current beliefs impact the vision.

Many successful people meditate on positive affirmations to help their vision become a reality. You can recite your vision over and over or make a simple audio recording of yourself walking through the goals. Either way, hearing yourself repeat the verbiage will help you focus on the positive outcome.

———

Let me suggest a practice that provides clarity for me at a gut level. Why do peers who meditate or pray on a regular basis find it so enlightening? One reason is because it's focused, uninterrupted time not invaded by texts, phone calls, celebrity gossip, or distractions.

By giving your mind some time "off the grid" to work behind the scenes, you may discover fresh ideas and surprising solutions.

The average person thinks 50,000 separate thoughts per day. On top of that mental clutter, we're bombarded by external distractions. If an individual is able to pull away, slow down, and *quiet their mind*, they're able to find a profound sense of peace. Isn't that what we all ultimately seek?

There's an old Zen saying that makes me chuckle and cringe at the same time: "You should sit in meditation for 20 minutes a day, unless you're too busy—then you should do it for an hour."

Don't have time to slow down? Plate's too full? Wrong. I create at least one "bonus" hour per day by not watching the news and not doing Facebook. It keeps me from getting "overstimulated" by media. Better yet, it allows me to replace one hour of negativity with one hour of positive life-affirming activity. If you reclaim just one hour of wasted time per day, it amounts to 365 bonus hours per year—the equivalent of nine, 40-hour workweeks.

(See the Appendix for the full text of John's Vivid Description of the Future.)

# BE INSPIRED

## Set Your Goals: *Measurable*

When I was a young man, I borrowed a set of Earl Nightingale tapes. One day while cruising in my Firebird Trans Am, I was half-listening as Earl talked about goal setting. Then something he said jumped out. "Every worthy goal ever set in the history of mankind has been achieved."

*What?* I couldn't believe my ears. I hit rewind (remember rewind?) and listened again and again. This man on the tape was telling me I had a guaranteed pathway for the rest of my life called goal setting. What I soon learned from personal experience was that 80 percent of my goals did come true merely by *writing them down*!

(The remaining 20 percent also came to pass but took additional hard work and perseverance in addition to writing them down.)

These goals didn't always happen exactly how I worded them, and they didn't always occur in the time frame I planned—but they *did* come true. My visioning on paper *did* become reality.

Over the decades, I've studied this remarkable linkage between setting tangible goals and seeing results. Today, this Legacy Map tool will help you cast a vision and live out a plan that can make every season of your life exceptional.

Looking back on my life, I realized that most of the time I got the things I really wanted. It's still the case today. When I set my mind on achieving something, and I apply my focus and energy, it usually happens.

Does it ever fail? Yes. When something doesn't work out, it's almost always because I became *distracted* by nonessential activity. The interruptions and demands of life shifted my attention onto areas of lesser significance.

Join me in creating and attaining a well-conceived vision of your stronger, smarter, happier, healthier, purpose-driven future self. It will serve you, your family, and your community in ways you can only imagine. We'll look at three kinds of goal setting—**Lifetime Goals**, **One-Year Goals**, and **Quarterly Targets**.

Ready? Let's consider the three goal-setting elements of your Legacy Map.

# Goal Setting >> LIFETIME GOALS

*"Always begin with the end in mind."*

That's good advice for road trips, work projects, marriages, careers—just about every activity, organization, or relationship you can possibly imagine.

This classic wisdom is from Stephen Covey, and it underscores the importance of being crystal clear on your desired Lifetime Goals. If you don't know (or care) where you're going, then your destination will be determined by random chance. And that's a roll of the dice at best.

This first step to beginning with the end in mind is answering an unusual but essential question: *"How old are you going to be when you die?"*

Before you blurt out a quick answer, realize that what we "say to our brain" has a powerful effect. You'll actually be telling your subconscious how long you want to live, planting the seeds of your own future. So don't be flippant; consider the ramifications of answering and be sincere.

I ask people to come up with a *specific* number, like 89 or 95. As Brian Tracy says, "Whatever we expect with confidence becomes our own self-fulfilling prophecy." I agree. In general, we usually tend to fulfill our own expectations, good or bad.

Got the number?

After you've decided how long you want to live, picture yourself exactly one year before that end point. For instance, let's say you picked age 90—one year before that would be age 89. (For simplicity, let's pretend you're the same age I am now, which is 60.)

Now, please visualize yourself 29 years from now at age 89.

Don't see yourself as sick or feeble, but as a healthy and vibrant 89-year-old *bon vivant*. If you know or admire someone in their 80s or 90s who is fit and active, imagine that's you. If they're still driving, still mentally sharp, still pleasant and fun to be with, imagine that's you. If they're productive and eager to learn, imagine that's who you are at 89!

For this exercise, you can even use a mental composite of several different seniors who each represent different aspects of your ideal future self.

In my case, I see the future me carving up a ski slope, riding my personal watercraft, and playing sports with my grandkids. I see myself active in business and adding value to the community. I see myself driving, traveling, and being deeply grateful for my life. I see myself spiritually, intellectually, and physically healthy.

One of my Lifetime Goals is to ski with my children and grandchildren at age 90 on a black diamond ski run in Aspen. This goal is specific; it explains when and where I am achieving the goal. It is achievable so long as I exercise daily and continue to ski challenging runs every year with my son. It is realistic because we know Klaus Obermeyer and others are still skiing well into their 90s.

Got the image? Good!

## LEAVE A LEGACY

Can a parade become a **Lifetime Goal?** One of America's most charming celebrations is the annual Fourth of July parade in Glen Arbor, Michigan. People of all ages line up to watch marching bands, fire trucks, and patriotic floats. Best of all, bicyclists also participate. That's where my client, Mike Brennan, comes in. His Lifetime Goal is to lead the Glen Arbor parade on his bicycle at age 100! Mike uses this vision as inspiration—not only for exercising daily but for pushing through challenging times.

He recently learned he has a form of cancer. Instead of shrinking from the prognosis, he funnels his energy into getting past the disease—always driven by his compelling vision of leading the parade at 100!

# One Year Left to Live.

Now that you have a positive image of your 89-year-old self, I need you to accept another construct to complete this exercise.

Pretend you've only got one year left to live.

Remember, you're 89 and according to your life span goal of 90, this is your final year on the planet. Because you're a goal setter, you're still active and vital. Because you're a person of character and values, you're humbled by having had such a long, productive life. When you originally set your age target as 90, you had some initial apprehension. But by now you're convinced about the power of the human mind and the efficacy of setting goals that allowed you to thrive.

Above all, you are truly thankful for how blessed your 89 years have been.

In this state of clarity and gratitude, you commit to being very intentional about what could well be the final year of your life. You do not take it for granted. In fact, you realize that you are a walking encyclopedia of life experience. You realize like never before that your remaining time is extremely valuable, and you're determined your final year will not be squandered.

At this point, I ask clients a number of key questions about their last 52 weeks on earth. For instance, I might start with your residence: *Where will you be living during this final healthy year? Do you still live in your current home, or have you moved south or west to a warmer climate?*

Years ago, my wife and I agreed we'd like a home on a lake because we both enjoy the water. So we put a picture of one on our vision board. Today, we have a lakefront home in Northern Michigan—and it all started by visualizing where we'd want to live during our final year.

The more specifically you can write about this future home, the better. For example: *Will you be hosting children and grandchildren during holidays? Or will you be going to their homes?* This exercise is about visioning, so details matter.

Now that we have your future home determined, let's discuss travel.

*Do you plan on visiting that spot you've always dreamed of? Or is there somewhere special you'll want to return to, a memorable location?* Remember, you are healthy, vital, and vibrant. You are not sickly; travel will be enjoyable. Ask yourself: *Will you travel with or without family? Are you going as a couple* (assuming you have a spouse)? *How long is the trip?* Some will take off for a few weeks; those with significant assets may take an extended trip. Be specific.

Now let's talk about your body and brain. *How are you staying in such amazing shape?* Describe your daily routine. *Does it include walking, biking, swimming, skiing, golf? Do you exercise, eat right, and challenge your intellect? Now that you have the freedom of time, how are you caring for your mind and body?*

Okay, we've visualized your dream home, adventurous travel, and the daily time dedicated to your health. The next question is: *How and where do you contribute to the community? Are you serving on boards, helping out at your church, temple, or mosque? Are you helping with a family business? Are you mentoring young leaders?* There are countless community programs like Winning Futures, iMatter for Kids, and Infinite Family that could use your wisdom.

This type of "others-focused" engagement will keep your mind sharp and give you a sense of purpose and meaning—both are essential to a healthy life. As ideas about your last year pop up, keep writing them down. Plan in advance how you'll be leveraging your time and wisdom; it's critical not only to this exercise, but to the quality of your life going forward.

Now think about your inner self. *What about your spiritual life? Is it important to you?* Perhaps you consider yourself a Christian like I do, but have never spent much time exploring your faith. Ponder the big questions of life: *Why am I here? What is my connection to others or the divine? Is there an afterlife?* Virtually everyone thinks about their own mortality when confronted by tragedy or the death of a loved one. But why wait for a funeral when you can do it now, in advance? Knowing you'll be gone in a year, *How are you living your faith? Are you praying each day? Are you active in a spiritual community? Reading great texts?* Again, consider how valuable your time is at this final stage and write down your spiritual intentions.

Next, we need to visualize what financial freedom looks like in terms of your wealth and assets. The amazing life you have described in the questions above is going to take money, perhaps more then you have today. Write down the ideal net worth you wish to have (not necessarily at age 89).

Don't be shy, write down the largest number you feel comfortable committing to.

Does this question strike you as odd or boastful? Choosing your dream income is similar to how you determined your life span. Obviously, no one *knows* at what age they will die, but it's essential to the exercise. The goal of living to a healthy and vibrant 90 years of age *requires* a leap of faith. Use that same faith to commit to a financial number. Don't worry about how you're going to get there right now. Just write out the maximum amount you can get your head around. Have faith, take a deep breath, and write it down.

————

The final priority to consider is rejuvenation time.

When we're younger, we're blessed with endless energy and stamina.

I remember working third shift for a while, and when I finished work at 8:00 a.m. on Saturday, I would often skip an entire sleep cycle and spend time pursuing my passions. I'd stay up having fun or completing chores and never bother to go to bed until late Sunday. As I aged, I soon learned the importance of planned rejuvenation time to recharge my batteries.

The ideal rejuvenation activity is different for each individual. In my case, it has several consistent characteristics. It occurs outdoors in nature, it involves physical activity, and it's ideally shared with others (but can be done solo). The final critical criteria is that all technology and work-related requests are turned off so I can be fully present and grateful for my time in nature.

Take a moment and think about your own rejuvenation activities—the ones that worked best. Ask yourself what you were doing, who you were doing it with, and what were the key elements that gave you energy. They could range from full-blown vacations to momentary mental escapes. Next, write down and prioritize those activities so they are planned and scheduled going forward. Leaving rejuvenation time to chance usually results in poor health or total burnout.

Many people picture the traditional retirement model as a form of rejuvenation. In reflection, this underlying belief is false. Endless idle time is not rejuvenation—it is boring, unproductive, and unhealthy. Remember, everything in moderation!

———

The final step in the process is to sit back and reflect on the life you have just described at 89. In this picture, you are healthy—physically, mentally, spirituality, and now financially, too. You are traveling. You are spending time with family and friends. You are assisting the community by sharing a lifetime of well-earned wisdom. At age 89, your life still has meaning and purpose.

If that's the case, why check out at 90?

If you could live beyond 90 and still be as healthy as you described above, would you want to break the century barrier? Remember, there's an ever-increasing chance that we can all live well past 100 thanks to exponential progress taking place right now in medicine and biotechnology.

Knowing that, do you want to push your number to 101?

Congratulations, you just added 11 years to your life!

## Time to Pick Your Top Six Priorities.

The next important key to mapping out your future is determining your top six priorities.

My personal priorities are **spirituality**, **health**, **relationships**, **calling**, **financial freedom,** and **rejuvenation**. These six have worked well for the majority of my clients over the years. But feel free to customize. For instance, some users who are not religious replace spirituality with personal development. Others replace the priority I describe as calling with career or community instead.

Above all, this is *your* Legacy Map, so use whatever heading suits you best.

# First, a Quick Word on Career vs. Calling.

Why do I personally use the word "calling" and not "career?"

Because my work is directly related to my larger purpose in life. It's a unique *conduit* for my unique *strengths* that adds unique *value* to the world.

As TV host, Steve Harvey says, "Your career is what you're paid for, your calling is what you're made for."

In her book, *Grit: The Power and Passion of Perseverance*, Angela Duckworth sums up this vital distinction. "Three bricklayers are asked, 'What are you doing?' The first says, 'I'm laying bricks.' The second says, 'I'm building a church.' The third says, 'I'm building the house of God.' The first bricklayer has a job. The second has a career. The third has a calling."

Consider the impact Baby Boomers could have on society if we all made the commitment to find our calling. How to start? As Bishop T. D. Jakes says, "If you can't figure out your purpose, figure out your passion. Your passion will lead you right into your purpose."

# Now Let's Return to Your Top Six.

Once your top six priorities are determined, you'll rank them in order of importance from 1 to 6.

Why limit your list to 6? Why not 10 or 20?

The answer is in the Verne Harnish classic *Mastering the Rockefeller Habits*. In it, Harnish tells the true story of a man named Ivy Lee.

Known for his work with the Rockefeller family and Andrew Carnegie, Ivy Lee is often called the "father of public relations." He was also a genius at helping companies enhance their performance. In a historic meeting with Charles Schwab, Lee unveiled his now-famous dictum of limiting and ranking goals.

In 1918, Schwab was one of the world's richest men and president of Bethlehem Steel. To gain advantage over his competitors, Schwab asked Lee to meet with his team. In just 15 minutes, Lee taught each executive a strategy for peak productivity. *At the end of each day, write down the six—and only the six—most important things you need to accomplish tomorrow. Rank them in order of their true importance. When you arrive tomorrow, concentrate only on the first task. Work until the first task is finished before moving on to the second task. Repeat.*

That's it. Productivity skyrocketed by 20 percent. (My friend and mentor Verne Harnish reduced the number from six to five—primarily for business use.)

———

Setting limits forces you to make tough decisions. "Basically, the more you try to do, the less you actually accomplish. This is a stark, inescapable principle we all live with." That's according to Chris McChesney, coauthor of *The 4 Disciplines of Execution: Achieving Your Wildly Important Goals.* He says, "Focusing on the wildly important means narrowing the number of goals you're attempting to accomplish." Along with fellow authors Sean Covey and Jim Huling, McChesney warns it's futile to try and change behavior in a "whirlwind"—an environment swirling with too many goals.

My friend Peter Thomas urges a similar regimen. "I focus by being goal-oriented. I have a thing called my MITs—my 'most important things'—and I move them ahead every single day. When I get up in the morning, they're the first thing I look at so I know what I'm doing that day. I set a goal, and that goal is my focus."

Billionaire Warren Buffet has a kindred principle. Called the 25-5 Rule, it requires us to zero in on our top five critical tasks and avoid the 20 runners-up "at all costs."

## John's Lifetime Goals

**Age: 103**

**6 PRIORITIES: *Spirituality, Health, Relationships, Calling, Financial Freedom, and Rejuvenation***

### 1. Spiritual
   a.  Intimacy with God - Surrender Daily
   b.  Be the thought leader that replaced retirement with intentional living
   c.  Modeling God's wisdom in my behavior & words

### 2. Health
   a.  165lbs / 16% BF / 33" waist
   b.  Fit / Firm / Active 7 days per week
   c.  Flexible, sober, daily stretching

### 3. Relationships
   a.  Married & deeply in love with Molly
   b.  Black diamond skiing w/ grandkids at 90
   c.  Valued role model to children without judgement of their life choices

### 4. Rejuvenation

    a.  6 months of rejuvenation time scheduled

    b.  Utilize Daily Alignment for energy maximization

    c.  (outdoors, activity based, disconnected, challenging, experiential)

### 5. Calling

    a.  Mastery of God's purpose for my life

    b.  Noted & sought after author & advisor

    c.  Living my Purpose & MTP

### 6. Financial Freedom

    a.  $5M value in multiple companies
        $2M income / $25K per day speaking

    b.  $20M net worth / no debt

    c.  Gift $200K annually

# Goal Setting >> ONE-YEAR GOALS

Throughout the book, I've reinforced the importance of thinking exponentially.

Before we move on to your One-Year Goals, let me go back and challenge your Lifetime Goals. Were they the product of *linear* or *exponential* thinking?

Even though the world is changing exponentially, our brains still tend to think in a linear, sequential manner. That means we visualize and predict our own ability to change (grow, improve, succeed, help others, etc.) in a linear way.

Doing that misses the true limitlessness of human potential. Unless we deliberately cultivate an exponential mindset, the Lifetime Goals we set for ourselves usually fall *below* the mark.

As we saw in Section 1, exponential thinkers are amongst us: people like Elon Musk, who wants to colonize Mars; Larry Page, who wants to reinvent the computer; Ray Kurzweil, who wants to reach singularity and live forever; Peter Diamandis, who wants to solve humanity's biggest problems, and many more.

These thought leaders are able to conceive and believe in an unlimited future by moving beyond linear goal setting and self-imposed limitations. Like them, we need a *belief shift* in what we think is possible as we project Lifetime Goals.

Once you've re-evaluated (and maybe expanded) your Lifetime Goals, let's tackle the One-Year Goals.

## Get Smart.

Most readers find this section easier because we've all created annual goals before. (If nothing else, we've all made New Year's resolutions!) Write down your current goals, utilizing the Legacy Map form on the next page. In case you're inclined to jump around, I strongly encourage you not to set your One-Year Goals until after you've completed the Lifetime exercise.

(I typically complete this process between November and February, so I'm looking at a typical 12-month calendar which seems to flow nicely. Depending on when you're completing this exercise, you can go from the current date until the end of the year, or you can look out 14 or 16 months as appropriate.)

Something that helps me set One-Year Goals is the well-known acronym S.M.A.R.T. It's been around forever and it's a nice grid to evaluate your goals.

- **Specific.** Generalized goals don't cut it. Be clear and specific. Answer the "W" questions. Who is involved? What exactly do I want to accomplish? Where will I do this? When will I do this?

- **Measurable.** Develop concrete metrics for measuring progress. How much? How many? How will I know when I've hit my goal? Being able to track your progress is essential to reaching goals.

- **Achievable.** Challenge yourself, but think about the obstacles. *Is the goal reasonable? Is it something you have control over?* Goals should be achievable, not impossible.

- **Realistic.** Dare to dream, but keep it real. Ask yourself tough questions. *Do I have the attitude, ability, and resources to reach this? Am I willing and able to do whatever it takes?*

- **Timely.** Without deadlines, there's no urgency. "Someday" won't work. Anchor a goal to a date, and your unconscious mind kicks in to reach it.

Big or small, short term or long term, you can always evaluate your goals through the five criteria of the S.M.A.R.T. acronym.

## LEAVE A LEGACY

One of my **One-Year Goals** was relational. When my mother passed away, I had no sense of closure. I didn't want that to be the case with my father. I wanted to show him I loved and appreciated him—while he was still healthy. I wrote this into my Lifetime Goals even before I had an idea of how I would accomplish it. Three years later, it came to me! I would take dad on an extensive driving trip to visit Civil War battle sites (**Specific**). He readily agreed, and we scheduled the date (**Timely**). My plan was to spend time together, share experiences, and have personal conversations—the in-depth kind that move beyond superficial chats (**Realistic**). Our trip began in Richmond, Virginia, and headed south down the Blue Ridge Parkway before ending up in Savannah, Georgia.

It was a huge success (**Measurable**). We had candid discussions with time to share what I admired about my father. I even had freedom to have "difficult" conversations; all in a healthy, affirming way (**Achievable**). Getting the concept down on paper was step one of what turned out to be a huge success. By the end of the trip, I had a wonderful sense of closure. Memories were made. Bonds were strengthened. Nothing was left unsaid. My advice—get it on paper!

As a coach, I've seen that modern executives, teams, and individuals (including me) suffer from a combination of two syndromes. First, trying to overachieve, and second, trying to accomplish everything right now.

Some of us flatter ourselves by believing we can "multitask"—even though research indicates it's a myth. Apparently, we are merely processing a lot of things in a parallel fashion.

In his popular blog, *Barking Up the Wrong Tree*, Eric Barker puts it bluntly, "We can't multitask—it makes us dumber, less productive, and ends up taking more time. It's just not how our brains work best."

Tests show multitasking significantly lowers performance in cognitive tasks compared with a sequential execution. Juggling more than one job at a time hinders overall performance but makes us feel better emotionally.

Don't fall for it.

"Human beings are genetically hardwired to do one thing at a time with excellence," says author Chris McChesney.

Do you hate stop-and-go traffic? So does your brain. Here's why—every time we stop-and-start while working on priority issues, it takes up to 20 minutes for our mind to fully reengage in our previous activity. This unfocused approach is allowable on menial tasks that require only minor thinking, but not for "deep work" like planning your legacy or adding value to society.

Barker explains, "Deep work is using your skills to create something of value. It takes thought, energy, time and concentration. Shallow work is all the little administrative and logistical stuff—email, meetings, calls, expense reports, etc."

In both our work life and our personal life, it's important to know the difference. In his book, *Deep Work: Rules for Focused Success in a Distracted World*, Cal Newport says, "Deep work is to focus without distraction on a cognitively demanding task, and shallow work describes activities that are more logistical in nature, that don't require intense concentration."

When we try to multitask or take a stop-start approach, we're "drowning in the shallows" while the world is valuing deep work more and more.

Knowing optimal styles of working and thinking will also help as you plot your Legacy Map. Check out Barker's blog (*bakadesuyo. com*) for more info on the practices I've touched on above, including links to supporting research.

## Who's on First?

If you saw my personal Legacy Map, you'd find my number one priority is "Spiritual" across each time frame. But that's just me; it's not mandatory that your priorities be the same across each time frame. Feel free to mix and match.

When you're setting your Lifetime Goals, I suggest you rank your six priorities in an *idealized* order. If you want "Relationships" to come first in the future, then list that first. It's not dishonest to rank priorities in terms of your *envisioned* future—you're just predicting the best possible future version of you.

However, when you're setting One-Year Goals, be practical and realistic. I tell clients to be brutally honest here. If "Career" is your number one priority *right now*, then list it that way. Don't pretend "Health" is number one if you're surviving on pizza and working 70 hours a week. Be sure that how you rank your priorities aligns with your daily reality.

The question here is not, what *should* matter, but what *does* matter?

Remember, priorities can easily be changed, so no pressure. Just ask yourself, "What am I really, truly going to make my first priority each day?"

You could say the Lifetime Goal is what's *envisioned,* the One-Year Goal is what's *achievable,* and the Quarterly Target is what's *executable.*

When I first began utilizing the goal-setting approach that evolved into the Legacy Map, my number one priority was my lifestyle and maintaining the freedom I enjoyed. So in that season, my goals aligned with that priority.

Later on, when I set my life span at 103, I made "Health" my top priority! If I didn't, I was never going to make it, or if I did, I'd be a broken-down geezer. Not a pretty picture. Finally, after I started exercising and caring for my body (annual physicals, healthy eating, exercise), I ranked "Spiritual Growth" as my number one priority.

Incidentally, this all evolved over a 20-year process, so don't feel the need to create the ideal plan overnight!

## John's One Year Goals

**Year: 2018**

### 1. Spiritual
   a. Daily sobriety & daily meditation
   b. 90 minutes on Daily Alignment (mental + physical + spiritual)

## 2. Calling

a. Finish & publish "Replace Retirement"

b. Package LM unique process & finish MVP for scalable business

c. Steelcase moves forward with proposal for LM process

## 3. Health

a. Daily fasting

b. Daily workout except free days (calisthenics & cardio)

c. Lower weight from 184lbs to 175lbs

## 4. Relationships

a. Plan two trips/visits annually with John & Katie

b. Plan 60th birthday trip with Molly

c. Support Molly on doctoral program & prioritize Molly time

## 5. Rejuvenation

a. 2 months scheduled rejuvenation time

b. Explore with Molly what defines her rejuvenation time

c. Limit email during free days

## 6. Financial Freedom

a. $350K revenue (coaching + speaking + Dogtopia)

b. Create budget discipline

# Goal Setting >> QUARTERLY TARGETS

Quarterly Targets are built around annual goals; in essence, you have four distinct quarters in the year to accomplish your goals. If you followed my advice earlier and kept your list of new goals for the year to a minimum, congrats! You now have time and space to accomplish your goals without overwhelming yourself.

There are two common roadblocks to reaching our goals:

- First of all, we tend to take on way too much at once. We are by nature an over-eager, overachieving bunch.

- Second, we're already working through a humongous list of important tasks each day. The items on this big list are usually not vision board goals, but must be done nonetheless.

Being distracted by a "whirlwind" of important tasks will derail us from achieving our goals. Chris McChesney cautions, "We don't have dragons swooping down and knocking us off our priorities. What we have are gnats getting in our eyes, and when we look back over the last six months, we haven't accomplished any of the things we said we were going to."

I'm sure you have phone apps and day planners and other tricks to organize your many responsibilities. And I'm equally sure tackling those to-do lists takes up most of your time. So when you pick even a *single* new target to accomplish in 90 days, it can be the proverbial straw that breaks the camel's back.

---

So let's take another look at what you've written down.

If you've ranked your six priorities and aligned specific annual goals to achieve those priorities during the next year, you now will drill down on the 90-Day targets you intend to address over the next quarter. There is space to have a maximum of three specific targets under each priority.

In theory, you could have as many as 18 distinct targets for the quarter grouped under your six priorities. But you could also have as few as six.

My advice is don't bite off more than you can chew. For example, let's consider health, my number two priority. From my own experience (and from watching countless others), I've learned that when it comes to setting health and fitness goals, most of us *overcommit* and *under-deliver*. Then, of course, we get discouraged and quit. Bill Gates correctly said, "Most people overestimate what they can do in one year and underestimate what they can do in ten years."

Sound familiar? We've all aimed too high and blown it. That's why four out of five gym memberships go unused. From diets to budgets, we've all set unreachable goals and become discouraged.

Like me, Greg McKeown believes in the power of "small wins." In my experience, small wins are the key to success when setting and reaching your Legacy Map goals. McKeown says, "When we start small and reward progress, we end up achieving more than when we set big, lofty, and often impossible goals."

Of course, there are always exceptions. My friend Paul Akers is a big-time goal setter and—this is much rarer—goal *achiever*. If this entrepreneur sets his mind on something, he will inevitably accomplish it. A child of Greek immigrants, Akers took his business from a small start-up in the family garage into a hugely successful product development company. Akers's business has prospered and expanded, even during economic downturns. In fact, he's never laid off an employee or cut a single salary.

You can see Akers's passion about "continuous improvement" in a series of free videos at *2secondlean.com*. I also highly suggest his books as a way to realize the benefits of being "lean" both in business (*2 Second Lean: How to Grow People and Build a Lean Culture*) and in achieving health (*Lean Health: Aging in Reverse*).

## Start, Stop, Keep.

Like Paul Akers, I am a lifetime goal setter. And over the years, I've shared an insight that's helped many reach their goals: *Don't start too many new goals in a year, or more important, in a quarter.* You can always add more later.

It's all about setting *achievable* yearly goals. To do that, you're going to start some new things, stop some old things, and keep doing some things that are working well. In his book, *Scaling Up,* Verne Harnish reinforced this Start/Stop/Keep concept.

Harnish tells leaders, "We recommend that all executives and middle managers have a Start/Stop/Keep conversation with at least one employee weekly." He suggests three simple questions to gather feedback and ideas: "What should we start doing? What should we stop doing? What should we keep doing?"

I have applied Harnish's model to my Legacy Map process. Again, using my number two priority (health) as an example, here's a typical model:

- Set one goal to START doing a new healthy habit.

- Set one goal to STOP doing an unhealthy habit.

- Set one goal to KEEP doing an existing healthy habit.

You get the idea.

- A "start doing" goal is like starting yoga classes, or starting to take vitamins, or starting to walk five miles a week. In my case, I started sending personal, handwritten "thank you" notes. I had always admired this form of courtesy, so I started writing at least one note each morning.

- A "stop doing" goal would be quitting a bad habit like smoking. When I gave up drinking alcohol, it was clearly a "stop doing" goal. Nowadays, I don't drink much soda pop as a rule—maybe one soft drink a week—so it would be relatively easy to cut out sodas entirely for a year.

- A "keep doing" goal is maintaining my current exercise program. I like the benefits of exercise—how it gives me energy, keeps me fit, and wakes me up more effectively than coffee. But the actual exercise is not enjoyable to me. So working out is a maintenance activity; I track it so I don't neglect it.

Again, feel free to mix and match. The trick is to only make commitments you can actually keep.

Each time we break a commitment to ourselves, we feel *guilty*. Eventually, we stop setting goals altogether because each flop is another blow to our self-esteem. With each broken promise, we're telling our subconscious, "I'm a person who doesn't keep commitments." We essentially program our internal computer with bad code.

Fortunately, as we saw earlier, we can reprogram our mind by setting and keeping goals. Unfortunately, deeply entrenched memories can rise up and prevail. When this happens, a single mistake (can you say Häagen-Dazs?) can feel like a permanent failure—and we begin to spiral down again.

Fortunately, there's a way to safeguard against this pattern, too. Again, I'm suggesting small, incremental, positive steps of making and keeping doable commitments until we totally overwrite old code with new code. Then one day, you'll be the next Paul Akers—able to accomplish anything you set out to do.

A Quarterly Target can be as simple as scheduling a vacation. For instance, I take an annual skiing trip with my son. I make planning the trip my Quarterly Goal for the fourth quarter and actually taking the trip my Quarterly Goal for the first quarter. Writing down this Quarterly Goal transforms a "nice idea" into a concrete strategy (book the flights, procure a rental home, etc.). Part of my Quarterly Goal is planning the trip in such a way that I can be fully engaged with my son and fully immersed in our activities together. I make sure in advance that I'll be able to focus my time and attention strictly on us—without distractions or competing obligations.

Planning and executing this ski trip is a good example of how a Goal doesn't have to be complicated or "big"—it just has to be important to you! Knowing this will help offset our natural human tendency to overcommit and under-deliver.

————

Let's review. My Quarterly Targets are 90-day chunks of my One-Year Goals. My Quarterly Targets are then broken down into my 30-day Focus Plan. From there, I further drive them down into Weekly and Daily Action Items.

Same rules apply that we used when setting One-Year Goals. (Using the Start-Stop-Keep grid, you could choose one "start doing" and one "stop doing" OR choose two "start doings" OR choose one "stop doing" and one "keep doing"—whatever combo works best.)

Remember, less is always better!

## John's Quarterly Targets

**Quarter: Q4 2018**

### 1. Spiritual
   a. Maintain sleep meditation before bed add 10 min morning
   b. 90 minute daily alignment
   c. Daily sobriety

**2. Calling**

    a. 1000 hard covers of RR book printed before 12/31/18

    b. Utilize Steelcase group to finalize & document the Intentional Living unique process

    c. Gain strategic partner alignment for investment & growth

**3. Health**

    a. Limit sugar & bread for balance of quarter

    b. Continue daily fasting weekdays

    c. Schedule knee MRI scan

**4. Relationships**

    a. Plan a trip or get together with Katie

    b. Schedule Christmas & spring ski trip with John

    c. Weekly walk with Molly in GR

**5. Rejuvenation**

    a. Enjoy fall colors and prepare for winter sledding

    b. Determine Molly's winter doctorial schedule & mine for sledding

    c. Enjoy 60th birthday celebration in Vegas with Molly

**6. Financial Freedom**

    a. Begin promoting RR presentation to secure 2 additional paid gigs

    b. Package the Intentional Living process for RIA market

    c. Fund book publishing

# Goal Setting >> 30-DAY FOCUS PLAN

The intention of the 30-Day Focus Plan is to further break down the Quarterly Targets into manageable chunks, or Milestones, providing greater focus on what is most important to accomplish. Similar to my earlier direction, I'm asking you to limit yourself to a maximum of three Milestones in the next 30 days.

In this short window, it's critical that we think carefully about how much time and mental bandwidth is available to work on what is likely important but less urgent. Accepting the whirlwind of life, I usually limit myself to one new or challenging area of improvement. My other two focus items are easier (yet still important) to-do's.

Keep your 30-Day Milestones simple. You may recall that one of my first successful daily rituals was journaling. Once I got over my initial reluctance, it went from being a chore to being a joy. Now it's a locked-in habit. One of my 30-Day Targets is similar to this, but different. I made it my declared goal to "Begin 20 minutes of daily writing." I would write each morning five days a week—usually in blog form. (My journaling time is a reflective mode; my writing time is a creative mode. I spend time doing both.) My long-term dream was to become a noted author. But that was too overwhelming! So I eased into it by writing something, anything, every day for 30 days. Soon, I was looking forward to my time spent writing, and it became a sustainable, energizing, lifetime habit. This example shows how living your legacy requires only two commitments—first, to "be inspired" (write down your goal), and second, to "manage your energy" (take action by doing something every day).

**1. October**

    a. Present investor pitch deck to 2 interested parties

    b. Daily meditation practice on work days

    c. Schedule Thanksgiving & Christmas

**2. November**

    a.

    b.

    c.

**3. December**

    a.

    b.

    c.

# MANAGE YOUR ENERGY

## Practice Your Habits: *Actionable*

You've heard the old saying, "It takes 21 days to develop a habit."

I don't buy it.

In my experience, it takes 90 days to develop a habit. And it looks like science is on my side. Phillippa Lally is a health psychology researcher at University College London. In a study published in the *European Journal of Social Psychology*, Dr. Lally and her team studied how long it actually takes to form a habit.

They found on average, it takes more than two months before a new behavior becomes automatic—66 days to be exact. Depending on how tough or complex the habit was (like doing 100 sit-ups versus drinking more water), it could take up to 254 days to lock in a new habit!

To set your Legacy Map expectations appropriately, figure it will likely take 90 days to build a new behavior into your life. (At *ReplaceRetirement.com* we offer our "Daily Alignment tool." Each morning you'll receive a reminder to take action on your daily habit. In the evening, we provide reinforcement as well as encourage you to express one thing you are grateful for each day.) During that time, give yourself permission to fail now and then, but develop strategies for quickly getting back on track. Understanding that habits are a process and not an event makes it easier to manage expectations and commit to making small, incremental improvements. Whether it takes 30 days or 300 days, it will require perseverance and grit, but it *will* be worth it!

---

All this begs the question: *what fuels transformative change?*

Not big, flashy breakthroughs, but modest, incremental advances. "Small wins are exactly what they sound like and are part of how keystone habits create widespread changes. A huge body of research has shown that small wins have enormous power, an influence disproportionate to the accomplishments of the victories themselves."

That's from Charles Duhigg's best-selling, *The Power of Habit: Why We Do What We Do in Life and Business*. He reinforces my belief that small repetitive wins become affirming patterns that encourage us to believe that even our biggest goals are doable given enough time.

An example from my own experience might be helpful. The first habit I intentionally acquired was journaling. My own father kept a daily journal, just like his father before him. My grandfather, James Watt Anderson, was an Arctic explorer and chronicled Canadian frontier life within the Hudson Bay Company. Born in 1893, he wrote the *Fur Trader's Story*, a historical novel published in 1961.

I began my first day with a blank journal and attempted to fill one page with my thoughts. At first, I just muscled through it, gritting my teeth. I repeated this ritual each morning, seven days a week, mostly out of obligation. But before I reached my goal of 90 days, journaling had actually become enjoyable. What had started as a struggle became rewarding, and it was easy and energizing to maintain this first daily habit.

Over time, I continued to gain Daily Alignment in my morning routine, but it all began with that first 90-day journaling commitment.

Why is that important?

If you established just one new habit every quarter, you would be adding four new habits each year. That's 40 in 10 years, and 80 new pro-active habits in 20 years! Essentially, you could transform yourself into an entirely new and improved person—making any future you chose to embark on a reality.

# Is Dramatic Change Really Possible?

It is if you're willing to put in the time. In his book, *Outliers: The Story of Success*, Malcolm Gladwell says, "If you work hard enough and assert yourself, and use your mind and imagination, you can shape the world to your desires."

But being great at something does not come cheaply or overnight. Gladwell states, "Researchers have settled on what they believe is the magic number for true expertise: 10,000 hours."

Gladwell stirred some controversy; subsequent clarification added that practice must be structured with steadily increasing levels of difficulty, etc. But the point remains—worthwhile change *is eminently possible* with enough determination. (Note: If that 10K number seems impossible to attain, think of it this way—by age 11, most American kids have viewed 10,000 hours of television.)

Even icons (like Mozart or Tiger Woods) who are born with unusual natural talent are not "automatically" great. In his book, *Talent Is Overrated*, Geoff Colvin says that aside from physical attributes that may provide an advantage, everyone can achieve world-class performance through (drumroll, please) "deliberate practice" in his or her chosen field—business, music, sports, etc.

What does deliberate practice mean? Colvin says it's "a habit that is *designed*, can be *repeated* a lot, is *highly demanding mentally*, and *isn't much fun*."

If that discourages you, take heart. Colvin says, "If the activities that lead to greatness were easy and fun, then everyone would do them and they would not distinguish the best from the rest. The reality that deliberate practice is hard...means most people won't do it."

Which means you'll stand out all the more.

Think about it—Gladwell and Colvin both suggest that given enough time and practice, we can become proficient at just about anything. So when I practice a habit for a quarter (or one year or a lifetime), I am rewriting the old software in my brain that tells me I'm a quitter with a *new* program that says I am disciplined and follow through on commitments to myself.

Here's the key: self-discipline comes from establishing Daily Alignment through habits. Habits as a rule require at least 90 days of continuous application without a break, ideally at the same time every day. Are you a morning person? As I said, my best and most productive time is the morning. So generally, my Daily Alignment activities (exercise, writing, praying, etc.) take place early and are bundled together.

Ganging them up into a single time slot creates what I call "stickiness."

For me, getting them done early means less chance to forget or default. Maybe for you, the best time will be over lunch or in the evening after work. You'll find your physical space and your rhythm as you go.

Either way, be encouraged because it will get easier and "stickier."

Charles Duhigg defines habits as what allow us to "do a thing with difficulty the first time, but soon do it more and more easily, and finally, with sufficient practice, do it semi-mechanically, or with hardly any consciousness at all."

Once someone sets a goal and internalizes it, they tend to grow "to the way in which they have been exercised, just as a sheet of paper or a coat, once creased or folded, tends to fall forever afterward into the same identical folds."

Here's a bonus. Ever since I implemented my first habit (journaling), I get the same nice "surprise" while applying any new 90-day Alignment. If the habit is *good for me*, something shifts inside and what starts as a chore or a bore soon becomes a reward! So hang in there. The new habit will reinforce good beliefs about yourself—producing confidence, satisfaction, and results.

I establish Daily Alignment each morning by exercising spiritually, physically, and mentally.

*Spiritually*, I pray, reflect, and read the Bible. *Physically*, I work out and eat a healthy breakfast. *Mentally*, I read from a quality book, journal, and write a personal note of gratitude for a relationship. Only after that do I open my email and answer business calls, etc.

I begin with what Stephen Covey called "Quadrant 2" activities (*important, but not urgent*). In my case, that means praying, reading, journaling, and working out. Once I open up to "Quadrant 1" activities (*important and urgent*) like emails, phone calls, and projects, it's off to the races for the rest of the day. For me, early morning is the easiest time to control; after that I'm at the mercy of planned and unplanned events. (I explain Covey's four quadrants in Section 7.)

Why do things in the same order? To reinforce what matters most—and gain Daily Alignment!

"Routine is one of the most powerful tools for removing obstacles. Without routine, the pull of nonessential distractions will overpower us." That's author and strategist Greg McKeown. "There is a huge body of scientific research to explain the mechanism by which routine enables difficult things to become easy."

Basically, as we repeat a certain task (journaling, exercise, etc.) the neurons make new connections. With repetition, the connections get stronger and easier to activate. That's the reason we can drive to work each day without checking MapQuest or use our smartphone without consulting a tutorial.

By sticking to this rhythm, I am reinforcing what I wrote down and prioritized as important. My goals align with my actions. But that's for *my* life, not yours. Just make sure your daily actions and behaviors align with *your* stated goals. And, no, I don't keep this routine perfectly, but that's okay. I deviate for various reasons (but very seldom). I'm striving for *compound growth* of Daily Alignment applied continuously toward a worthy Lifetime Goal.

Like Mark Twain said, "Continuous improvement is better than delayed perfection." So don't beat yourself up if you slip.

## John's Daily Alignment

**My Daily Alignment habit is . . .**

Blog or write 20 minutes daily

# MANAGE YOUR ENERGY

## Be Responsible: *Accountable*

Who was the first mentor?

In Homer's *Odyssey,* Mentor is the trusted friend of Odysseus left in charge of the king's household during his absence. In the same poem, Athena disguises herself as Mentor to "guide and advise" Odysseus's son in his search for his father.

Today, the words mentor and coach are often used interchangeably. But they are different roles that can overlap. A *coach* gives specific, targeted instruction on how to enhance performance in a particular area (sink more putts, close more deals, etc.). The results are measurable. A *mentor* gives broad, "big picture" advice on life-building skills (be more creative, leave a legacy, etc.). The results occur over your lifetime and cross personal and professional lines.

If you want to achieve your goals, have a brighter future, and leave a lasting legacy behind, having some form of mentoring/coaching accountability relationship is absolutely essential.

Without outside help, it's hard (almost impossible) to turn good intentions into permanent lifestyle changes. In other words, how do you get stuff to stick? Two approaches work well.

One is to have a flesh-and-blood coach or accountability partner. An accountability partner is a valuable relationship, and I have many of them. However, an accountability partner may be only partially engaged in your Legacy Map. On the other hand, a coach *accelerates* the process because they can focus on your unique goals and vision. I recommend having both a coach and an accountability partner, if possible.

The other approach is to have an automated tool as your accountability partner. This affordable, practical alternative is almost like having your own personal assistant helping you stay true to your commitments and course. Perhaps like me, you've used a Fitbit or other technology-based accountability device and found surprising success. I can testify that utilizing them has helped me stay true to my vision and journey.

Based on my own good outcomes with interactive monitoring technology, we offer a couple of options for you at *ReplaceRetirement. com.* My partner and I have developed a simple text-based tool that prompts you each morning to practice your Daily Alignment. In the evening, it checks in with you again, prompting you to be grateful for one thing during the day.

Additionally, I became an owner and partner in a company called VizBe that designs ways to help you "achieve stickiness" and reach your goals. Our team created this system for the workplace to help managers and leaders engage their employees' "whole self" at work. Here's the bonus. It works great for Legacy Maps, too! (Access the resources at *VizBe.com.*)

The VizBe tool is a foundational framework you can use to set your Legacy Map goals (with some minimal adaptation). You'll find more information at *ReplaceRetirement.com* on how to use our automated tool.

# Spurring Each Other On.

I've been coaching clients for almost 20 years, both in teams and one-on-one. Looking back, I most enjoyed the one-on-one coaching because of the growth that happened for the individuals *and* for myself. There is *leverage* in teaching someone else what you are learning and applying yourself. Likewise, you gain *confidence* while applying tools you developed for others on yourself.

Around 2007, I started a multi-year coaching relationship with a client—meeting monthly one-on-one. During this process, he and I both grew significantly and were forever changed by the experience.

Because of that positive outcome, I sought out a parallel process with Michael Berger, one of my Entrepreneurs' Organization (EO) forum members. We established a monthly four-hour session to keep us accountable to our personal Legacy Maps. We have remained consistent with this process, meeting annually to review our past year and to establish our goals for the next 12 months.

Each *quarter*, we meet to score the past 90 days and then establish the next 90-Day Targets. Each *month*, we meet to review progress and establish a maximum of two to three Milestones. This 30-Day Focus Plan is designed to drive the most important targets for the quarter. Each *week*, I review my progress and establish no more than three action Items for the next week, and then score myself at week's end. Each *night*, I send out an email updating my accountability partner on my Daily Alignment, using the same format as above.

## LEAVE A LEGACY

When it comes to setting goals, fewer truly is better! Michael Berger is an Entrepreneurs' Organization (EO) forum mate of mine. About five years ago, I started meeting with him monthly. In the early stages of the process, Berger—like the majority of my new clients—set multiple Quarterly Targets within each Annual Goal to accomplish every 90 days. Like so many goal setters (myself included), Berger was trying to start too many new things in a short period of time. This eagerness set him up for frustration and disillusionment when he failed to meet his objectives. Over time, he heeded my advice to set fewer goals, and he eventually committed to setting only one goal per priority.

This insight on Berger's part is in fact the best way to set new goals. My only adjustment is to encourage setting a new goal while reinforcing existing ones. Too often, we forget to reinforce a good habit we've developed (like working out three days a week), and when something comes up, we fall off the wagon. Berger and I have both learned the value of tracking goals or healthy habits that we don't want to slack off on to make sure we don't neglect them. In my case, I actually reward myself for keeping my existing commitments.

Don't think you have to copy my process to be successful. Every person will have a unique accountability relationship with its own rhythm. But make sure to check our website to access the Daily Alignment tool.

# The Power of Partners.

I've made the Legacy Map available to you as a free PDF at our website (*ReplaceRetirement.com*). You can download it and utilize the outline contained in this book to complete the form on your own. However, I realize from my own experience that *reading* about a process and *completing* the process are two different things!

That's why I recommend a living, breathing accountability partner or a technology-based cyber-partner to keep you engaged and on track.

Better yet, why not both?

Once you've plotted your Legacy Map, you (with the help of your accountability partners) can begin reaching meaningful, long-term goals that won't get forgotten or neglected like all those broken New Year's Eve resolutions.

Remember, all change (positive or negative) comes down to rewiring your brain. And that's not an easy or overnight process. Today, people often describe me as "disciplined." But years ago (back when I was partying pretty hard), that would have been the last definition anyone—including myself—would ever apply to me.

As long as I saw myself as an undisciplined, out-of-control person, I remained stuck in that rut. I lived up to my own negative self-image. Today, without boasting, I can honestly call myself a disciplined person. Changing the way I saw myself and—more importantly—changing my *daily habits* were watershed moments. But I could have never done it without the systematic encouragement and discipline I obtained from having active and involved peer reinforcement.

Like you, I sincerely wanted a better future. But we cannot reach our long-term goals unless we change our short-term habits. And that's done one day at a time.

So get a partner. Get a device. Check out Legacy Map and VizBe. And connect with them daily! As John Maxwell said, "You will never change your life until you change something you do daily. The secret of your success is in what you do daily."

Being accountable to someone—or something—every day will keep you on track.

In Olympic archery, the target is 86 yards away. The bull's-eye is less than five inches in diameter, but medalists must place a dozen arrows inside it. Now imagine if there were no targets. Without something to aim at, even the best archers would be shooting arrows in all directions, hoping to hit something.

In life, the Legacy Map supplies the bull's-eye.

> *"There are seven days in the week and 'someday' isn't one of them."*
>
> —ANONYMOUS

# YOU'RE WAY TOO SMART TO RETIRE

## HOW RETIREMENT CAN SHORTEN YOUR LIFE, EMPTY YOUR POCKETS, AND SHRINK YOUR BRAIN.

*"Sooner or later I'm going to die, but I'm not going to retire."*

—MARGARET MEAD

*"You only retire from jobs you're not enamored with. I love what I do. I want to keep doing it until I can't get out of bed to do it."*

—MORGAN FREEMAN

# Making a U-Turn.

A new word has been added to the American vocabulary.

The word is "unretirement," and it's long overdue.

"We definitely see evidence that retirement is fluid," said Kathleen Mullen, a RAND senior economist and coauthor of its American Working Conditions Survey. "There's less of the traditional schedule: work to a certain age, retire, see the world. We see people lengthening their careers."

More and more people over 65 are dumping the traditional retirement model and forging new second-half careers. And they're making this U-turn in unprecedented numbers. A recent survey from RAND Corporation found nearly 40 percent of workers over 65 had previously retired and voluntarily *returned to work*.

In 2018, *The New York Times* profiled a successful critical care nurse who retired after 38 years on the job. At 66, she had a healthy body, a healthy 401(k), and no mortgage debt. Her retired husband was equally well off. They were both ready for a life of full-time idleness.

But her retirement only lasted three months. In her article, "Many Americans Try Retirement, Then Change Their Minds," Paula Span recounts how the highly skilled health-care professional found "days spent organizing recipes and photos, and lunching with friends, proved less engaging than expected." Like many talented retirees, she was disillusioned by a life without purpose. But there's a happy ending. Span says the nurse is "back at work in a part-time position she designed for herself."

She replaced retirement with purposeful living.

Span quotes Dr. Nicole Maestas, an economist at Harvard Medical School. "It looks like something people are doing intentionally…It's much more about a choice."

People are living longer, with more to offer at 65 than previous generations. And they're not content to become irrelevant. Dr. Maestas explains why people are un-retiring in droves. "You hear certain themes: A sense of purpose. Using your brain…Another key component is social engagement."

Is this trend because retirees are running out of cash? Paula Span refutes that notion. "Earning money, while welcomed, rarely proved the primary incentive."

The *Times* article describes another professional who'd saved enough to feel economically secure. But shortly after retiring, she said, "I felt like I was free-floating, bobbing along on the ocean…I felt very ungrounded." In my experience as a coach and advisor, this kind of unexpected negative reaction to leaving the workforce is all too common. In this case, the retiree became reclusive and required prescription antidepressants.

Three years ago, she took a part-time job supporting government researchers. Now 69, she enjoys adding value to society and has zero plans to retire. "As long as somebody wants me, I have a lot to contribute," she said.

And so do you.

# Stop Working, Start Dying.

Sadly, there's another gang with an opposite view. These workers can't wait to retire and kiss work goodbye. It doesn't make sense to me, but they are counting the days until they can punch out, sign off, kick back, hang loose, dial down, and twiddle their thumbs.

It's like an on/off switch gets flipped inside their head. Maybe it happens when government benefits kick in. Or when their company offers a buyout. But whenever an active person shuts it all down and becomes a couch potato, it's bad news. To trade a life of being mentally engaged and productive for a life of playing pickle ball is a recipe for dementia. Or maybe even premature death. Quitting too soon hurts your chances for a long, happy life. That's according to an article (ominously titled "Early Retirement, Early Death?") by Daniel DeNoon. He reports on a famous study of Shell Oil employees showing workers who retired at age 55 died significantly sooner than those retiring at 65. Even worse, people who retired at 55 were 89 percent more likely to die in the 10 years after retirement than those who retired at 65.

We usually don't associate retirement with depression and worsening health. But a Bloomberg article called, "Retirement Will Kill You" makes the link. "Researchers at the Institute of Economic Affairs in the U.K. recently identified 'negative and substantial effects on health from retirement.' Their study found retirement to be associated with a significant increase in clinical depression and a decline in health…"

And if retiring doesn't make you croak, it might make you sick.

A Dutch psychologist named Ad Vingerhoets has coined the term "leisure sickness" to describe a condition where retirees suffer from symptoms of illnesses brought on merely by having nothing to do.

Teddy Roosevelt said, "The best prize that life has to offer is the chance to work hard at work worth doing." Research now suggests Teddy was more correct than he knew.

Isn't it ironic? Right at the time when workers typically have the most experience, most connections, and most resources, they're putting their lives in limbo. Right when they have maximum abilities and maximum free time to really make a difference, they hit the pause button.

I'm asking you *not* to be that person. Don't buy into the myth of a carefree retirement. Many retirees I know are bored stiff. Their world is shrinking, their brains are shrinking, their nest egg is shrinking.

Don't be like them. Don't disappear into the Sunshine State.

## The Florida Syndrome.

As a longtime Michigander, I grew up hearing the term "snowbirds." It described thousands of my fellow northerners who escaped our freezing temps by visiting Florida. Each winter, they packed up the family and headed south for a week of blessed relief, always dreaming of the day they could retire and move there permanently. For generations of workers, this goal of living out their golden years on a golden beach was the reward they lived for.

Unfortunately, this migration didn't always turn out as planned. In fact, in many cases, their retirement years were a downhill slide into depression.

Author and philosopher Walker Percy remained busy speaking, writing, and winning awards until his death at age 74. Before he passed on in 1990, Percy predicted today's unhappy senior citizens. In an interview with Scott Walter for *Crisis* magazine, Percy noted the modern concept of retirement is so "prosaic, safe, and comfortable" that it virtually guarantees a late-life crisis.

To explain why traditional retirement is so often disappointing, Percy referred to a then-recent discovery called the "Florida Syndrome." Percy said, "A psychiatrist in St. Petersburg studied a lot of good people who did the right American thing—worked hard for 30 years, saved their money, retired, and went to live in this American Eden in Florida (or Southern California or Phoenix). They feel entitled to be rewarded for a life of toil, usually pretty dreary. After 30 years, they go to Florida, and a very large percentage gets depressed, gets disoriented, and feels terrible—so bad that a lot of them move back…"

The doctor Percy referred to was Dr. Dean Rotondo, who says that instead of finding Nirvana, retirees often face isolation, depression, and boredom. That's especially true for "snowbirds" (or anyone else) with delusions that a blissful paradise is waiting for them after a life of work.

"I call it the Florida Syndrome," says Dr. Rotondo, director of neurological studies at Fair Oaks Hospital in Delray Beach, north of Miami. "It's the reality of Florida versus the fantasy." According to his research, stress-related ailments, such as depression and chronic anxiety, are the most common symptoms. A native New Yorker, Dr. Rotondo says, "I came here thinking that if I had a problem, I would just go to the beach. Well, you can only go to the beach so much. When people come down here and find all the problems they left behind—what's left is a lot of disillusionment and irritability."

This mistaken idea that quitting work and dropping out of society will somehow bring happiness and satisfaction is persistent. And false. In his interview, Walker Percy said it's the "dreariness" of ordinary, unfulfilling jobs that leads workers to fantasize about a better life after retirement. And that dreariness will extend right into retirement if we're not intentional—if we don't have a carefully planned, goal-oriented strategy for our own lives.

Percy added, "From what I observe, even with the huge consumption in this country, an awful lot of people are very unhappy, find life very dreary, and move a lot—all the time. I know a couple—both of them over 70—who move from one condominium to another, looking for a different golf course."

———

Around 3,000 years ago, the author of *Proverbs* declared, "Where there is no vision, the people perish." It's still true—for nations, companies, and individuals.

## LEAVE A LEGACY

In the Environmental Protection Agency, the Senior Environmental Employment (SEE) Program has been around for more than 30 years. It offers a wide variety of jobs for retired and unemployed Americans age 55 and over. They can share their expertise with the EPA, remaining active using their mature skills to support different environmental programs. In a similar vein, through the Agriculture Conservation Experienced Services (ACES) program, experienced workers, age 55 and over, help employees provide technical services in support of conservation. Available positions span a variety of skillsets and educational levels. Both of these agencies offer job applications through the National Older Worker Career Center (NOWCC).

Without a vision for the future that includes staying active and helping others, life after your first-half career soon becomes a meaningless blur—what Einstein called a "hopeless dreariness." If you're not building a legacy day-by-day, the weeks and months can drag by like a monotonous exercise in futility.

Florida reporter Diane Lade described a typical retired couple in the Sunshine State, "He is sick of golf, bored with cards, and sometimes finds himself too tired for his morning walk—even after 10 hours of sleep. She misses the grandkids, hasn't met anyone she can really talk to, and sometimes finds herself feeling very lonely—even though she now sees her retired husband all day, every day, and is surrounded by people her own age."

Does that sound like a good way to spend 20, 30, or 40 years to you?

Me neither. The Florida Syndrome is the polar opposite of the rewarding, challenging, exciting life I'm advocating—in *whatever* state you choose!

Dr. Rotondo says, "Among the symptoms: increased irritability, anxiety, depression, severe loneliness and indecisiveness…When our expectations aren't being met, even a simple decision like deciding which supermarket to go to can become a major argument between husband and wife."

Give me a break. Retirees who have sacrificed and saved for decades need to wake up and smell the orange juice *long before* they sell their home and move to a retirement condo on the back nine somewhere. Otherwise, their dreams of leisure and freedom from responsibility will be dashed in about one month.

This shouldn't be a surprise. We're not wired up to stagnate. We're wired to accomplish things. And that wiring doesn't change when we hit a magic birthday.

Here's the kicker: whether a senior is just barely scraping by or has amassed a huge financial portfolio, the *same rules apply*. Money will not insulate you from Florida Syndrome (or Palm Springs Syndrome, Santa Fe Syndrome, etc.). Chasing any false version of the American Dream will not satisfy. Only a purpose-driven life of meaningful, others-centered activity will make you wake up each morning and feel excited about getting out of bed.

## Hollywood Gets It Right.

"There's no such thing as an ending; just a place where you leave the story."

That's a line from a movie I suggest you watch. In 2012, *The Best Exotic Marigold Hotel* was a surprise box office hit. It features a group of elderly Brits who plan to stretch their pensions by moving to India. Of course, the rundown residence is far less luxurious than advertised, but the retirees form friendships that make up for the culture shock.

A spirited 2015 sequel, *The Second Best Exotic Marigold Hotel*, brought back most of the original cast. In this film, the hotel's young owner (played by Dev Patel) flies to San Diego to attract an American investor (played by Daniel Strathairn). To the hotelier's surprise, Strathairn's character challenges active seniors to flourish. His enlightened approach echoes my goal for you. "The mature years are an opportunity for travel, for further education, for different work situations. In a word—an opportunity for life. And for passing on the value of that life to others."

To the movie's further credit, Judi Dench plays a 79-year-old widow who boldly re-enters the workforce by starting a job as a fabric buyer for an international company. The position involves considerable travel and responsibilities. After some soul searching, she *replaces retirement with intentional living.*

In real life, the 83-year-old Dench also refuses to retire. "It's the rudest word in the dictionary," she says. "And 'old' is another one. I don't allow that in my house. And being called 'vintage.' I don't like any of those old words. I like 'enthusiastic.'"

Her 64-year-old costar, Lillete Dubey, agrees. "You may be 60 or 70, but life never stops surprising unless you let it."

## Give Me Liberty.

Quick—what's on the back of a half-dollar coin?

If you said "the Liberty Bell," you're probably a Baby Boomer. The so-called Franklin half-dollar was only minted from 1948 to 1963.

As Boomers, the idea of liberty was reinforced during our formative years by parents who fought and sacrificed in WWII. We're products of their struggles and hardships, and the self-sufficiency they modeled is ingrained in us. Our independent streak runs deep, so when government, business, or society suggests (or dictates) that we're not capable of being independent, it grinds at us.

One way we retain our personal liberty and independence is by contributing our skills to the nation's economy (and to future generations) throughout our entire lives. If we continue working and creating value in some form, we can avoid relying on government agencies, bureaucracies, or family members to support us.

When society tells a person they've lost value due to advancing years, that person can accept it and surrender, or fight back by proving their worth in the marketplace. The poor soul who believes the lies about aging and drops out of the working world will often feel depressed, frustrated, and angry.

That's why maintaining our personal liberty is essential.

If you agree, your next logical step is to *defend* and *extend* that independence throughout the balance of your life. It's not only part of our birthright; it's the oxygen of a healthy mind, body, and spirit. See it as the *mental* independence to create value for yourself and others. See it as the *physical* independence to go places and experience the joy of living in all stages of life.

I warn you—independence won't be easy and you'll be swimming upstream. Public opinion on the subject of retirement and dependence on Big Government largesse is firmly entrenched. And it caters to the worst in human nature.

Thomas Jefferson said, "The natural progress of things is for liberty to yield and government to gain ground."

How's that working out? H. L. Mencken was right when he said, "Most people want security, not liberty."

It's that simple. So stay strong. Stay busy. Stay useful. Stay free.

# A Brief History of Retirement.

As you can guess, I am *not* looking to retire my skills or end my contribution. Just the opposite—I'm actively seeking out (and inventing) opportunities to maximize my usefulness and value to a ripe old age. Looking back, it's been this proactive approach to business and life that's given me the greatest sense of well-being.

Curtailing my drive to create value for others would drastically diminish my sense of significance—regardless of chronological age. Which raises the question, Why *do* we retire at 65?

Back in 1889, Chancellor Otto von Bismarck made Germany the first nation to adopt a social insurance program. Participation was mandatory and contributions were taken from workers and employers. The initial age of eligibility was set at 70 (later reduced to 65) back when the average life expectancy was 45 to 50 years—meaning most Germans would never live to receive benefits!

This cynical misdirection neutralized the Marxist agitators who were threatening to woo away German workers, but it also pushed eager, competent workers into a state-supported unemployment. "Bismarck was no dummy," says Mary-Lou Weisman of *The New*

*York Times.* "Hardly anyone lived to be 65 at the time, given that penicillin would not be available for another half century. Bismarck not only co-opted the Marxists, but set the arbitrary world standard for the exact year at which old age begins and established the precedent that government should pay people for growing old."

In 1935, President Franklin Delano Roosevelt copied our current Social Security from Bismarck as part of his much-vaunted New Deal. Like the Germans, American workers would now have a portion of their wages deducted to pay for their own old-age insurance—*if* they were lucky enough to live that long.

The US even followed Germany's lead and selected 65 as the eligible age—three years beyond the life span of a typical American at that time.

———

Instead of being a golden parachute, state-sponsored retirement was designed to be a brief safety net for the few lucky souls who outlived the national average.

Knowing the dubious origins of today's retirement model, does it strike you as a catalytic mechanism to: (1) drive a greater sense of freedom and independence; or (2) drive people into dependence and diminishing value? I believe it triggers the latter, becoming a sort of death knell to many of our peers. In my experience, when people opt for retirement, their creativity, confidence, and mental sharpness drop significantly and rapidly. They seem less able to solve problems and less willing to take risks.

That's not to say everyone caves in; some do, in fact, replace retirement with intentional living and enjoy happy, active, engaged lives into their 80s, 90s, and beyond. But sadly, that seems more the exception than the rule.

## You're Too Smart to Retire.

The old formula wasn't exactly rocket science—*Work until you retire. Then relax until you die.* For our parents (and many of our peers), that meant accumulating enough wealth between "hired" and "retired" to live out their final years without working.

But that model contains two fatal flaws. First, it tacitly implies that working is a negative, and indolence is a positive. Second, it equates happiness with leisure.

Trust me; I enjoy relaxing as much as anyone. But I maintain that a rich, joyful, abundant life is not dependent on "doing nothing." Quite the contrary, it relies on staying busy and creative and contributing, especially in your later years.

The good life doesn't start at 55 or 65 or any other birthday. It starts the day you realize your purpose in life and begin moving toward it. Mark Twain put it this way, "The two most important days of your life are the day you were born and the day you find out why."

Like most Boomers, I grew up hearing people say, "If I just stick it out at GM or Ford (or IBM or Blue Cross or whatever) for 30 years, I can finally enjoy myself." Sadly, some of them died early, missing the whole point of life, which is to enjoy the journey, not just the destination. Others who *did* make it to their retirement party were disappointed when the fairy tale they worked for all those years turned out to be boring and unfulfilling.

Another movie, *About Schmidt*, makes this point. An insurance salesman named Warren Schmidt (played by Jack Nicholson) retires. Planning to see America, he and his wife purchase a Winnebago. But days pass and Warren just sits in front of the television, bored and feeling useless. We gain insight into his disappointing retirement in a letter he writes, "Relatively soon, I will die. Maybe in 20 years, maybe tomorrow, it doesn't matter. Once I am dead and everyone who knew me dies too, it will be as though I never existed. What difference has my life made to anyone? None that I can think of. None at all."

Schmidt worked 30 years in a safe, predictable career that kept him busy, but unfulfilled. Now in retirement, he does the kind of soul-searching I routinely ask my clients to do. He asks, "What in the world is better because of me?"

Don't misunderstand. Delayed gratification is a good character trait. But it does *not* mean delaying happiness while you grind it out at a job you don't love.

A Gallup poll showed that 70 percent of Americans either hate their jobs or are completely disengaged. Even workplace perks—free lunches, nap rooms, ping-pong—are not alleviating the anger and boredom. According to the survey, many describe their work life as "merely trying to survive each day at the office."

This antipathy for work has produced a pair of destructive twins. In the short term, we're living for the *weekend*. In the long term, we're living for *retirement*.

The average American spends 90,000 hours at work. It's critical you do something you love, that you discover a "calling" and not just a "job."

What's the difference? Briefly, a calling is about passion and purpose; a job is mostly about a paycheck. Your unique calling is what you were born to do. It's what you dream about because it brings you energy and satisfaction.

And it's what you should be pursuing your entire life—first *and* second half.

This book is aimed at folks over 50. But it's applicable to anyone. Truth is not age dependent. If you want to live a long, healthy life, find the sweet spot where you can contribute with a big grin on your face right up until the end.

One person who did *exactly* that is changing the lives of thousands of inner-city students with the invaluable gift of art. She took the skills she learned in her first-half career (her job), combined them with her passion for public service (her calling), and crafted a second-half lifestyle that's making an impact. And she will never retire from doing it.

## LEAVE A LEGACY

Many people are passionate and articulate at pointing out what's wrong or missing in society. Very few actually do something about it.

Carol Hofgartner is one of those rare people who identified a challenge and had the courage to pursue a solution. I met Carol back in the early '90s, when I owned Gorman's Business Interiors. She worked as a designer at one of our large, corporate office furniture clients. For career day, Edison Elementary school invited her to speak about careers in architecture. She was shocked when the students told her that their school no longer held art classes. Hofgartner knew that art classes can improve overall academic achievement and can keep kids engaged, especially in under-resourced schools. Like many others, she identified a problem. But instead of simply complaining, she acted. Fueled by her purpose and vision, she left the security of her job to launch "Art Road"— a nonprofit dedicated to providing fully funded art education to Detroit elementary students.

Despite Carol's talent and enthusiasm, Art Road was far from an overnight success. Initially, she wore all the hats as art teacher, fundraiser, and administrator. Early on, she approached entrepreneurs like myself for advice and direction on how to best serve this worthy cause. What she didn't know she learned by doing. Over time, she attracted other skilled teachers and volunteers to support the work. She learned how to network and grow her influence. She learned where to invest time—finding funders whose values and beliefs aligned with her mission.

Carol Hofgartner's commitment to her vision and goals has paid off. And today, her dream of Art Road (*artroadnonprofit.org*) brings art classes to over 1,600 students in four schools. And their world-class model is spreading!

# Finding Your Calling (at Any Age).

In 1941, Earl Nightingale was one of 15 surviving Marines on the *USS Arizona* during the attack on Pearl Harbor. After the war, he became a highly respected writer and radio personality on the subject of character development and meaningful existence. He was famous for his snippets of wisdom:

> *"If the grass is greener on the other side of the fence, it's probably because it's getting better care."*

> *"Success is not a matter of luck or circumstance. It's not the breaks you get or who you know. It's sticking to commonsense principles anyone can master."*

When I worked at IBM, they offered a lending library of personal development books on tape (remember cassettes?). One day I checked out Nightingale's 1956 classic, *Lead the Field*. Plugging it into my player, I discovered the magic word in life was not abracadabra, but "attitude." In the decades since, I've listened to the book over 100 times. In it, Nightingale explains that we're born into a certain socioeconomic level, and the most common goal is to rise just a little above it.

For many, that slight increase is how they define success. But why settle for that? The beauty of being at the top of the socioeconomic pyramid is that it's the first place the sun hits every morning and the last place it sets every evening. I ask you point-blank, "If the air is cleaner, and the view is better, and it's not crowded—why not go up there?"

———

Our *attitude* determines our *actions*—and when we accept responsibility for our attitude, we accept responsibility for our entire life.

Nightingale once said, "We are all self-made—but only the successful will admit it."

Another way to define success was created by Abraham Maslow when he outlined his famous hierarchy of needs in 1943. These motivating impulses are often depicted as a pyramid. On the lowest level are "biological and psychological" needs—air, food, drink, shelter, warmth, sex, and sleep. On the very top are "self-actualization" needs—realizing personal potential, self-fulfillment, personal growth, and peak experiences.

All of us have certain fundamental needs, and we try to meet them in a particular order. In his book *Peak: How Great Companies Get Their Mojo from Maslow*, Chip Conley simplifies those needs into three levels. At the bottom are safety and security, in the middle is recognition, and at the top is self-actualization.

Here's how that applies to your work life. At the bottom (in a job), you get safety and security; the reward is financial. In the middle (in a career), you get recognition and acknowledgment; the reward is self-esteem. At the top (in a calling), you get purpose and meaning; the reward is self-actualization.

Conley recounts how the ascending levels of the pyramid first represent survival needs, then social approval, then the ideal state of fulfilling your life's calling.

After Chip introduced me to this three-tiered concept, I quickly integrated his ideas into my coaching (check him out at *chipconley.com*).

Nightingale, Maslow, and Conley concur on one key concept—virtually everyone has a conscious (or subconscious) desire to move up the pyramid toward self-actualization—the level of *doing what matters most* with our talents and passion. This plays out differently for individuals. Some achieve it by mentoring others or expressing creativity in the arts. Others achieve it by inventing technology, or modeling leadership, or exhibiting compassion.

Whatever the unique expression—in a corporate setting or in a remote medical clinic—self-actualized people operate in their "calling" by doing all they are capable of while pursuing the purpose that's most important to them.

I'm living proof this can happen. I have a calling, but it's also a wonderful career. I make good money, people affirm me, and clients refer me to others. I get tons of ego strokes, I have job security, and companies want my services. (I not only worked full tilt through the 2008 recession, my revenue actually increased.) Bottom line? Pursue your *calling*. Follow your *passion*.

## For All the Right Reasons.

Somebody once asked me to define self-actualization. I replied, "Looking in the mirror and being pleased with the person looking back at you."

Everyone defines self-actualization differently.

Most high-achieving Boomers are gratified to achieve a career that brings a dose of fame and fortune. It feels great for a while. But then in the second half of life, it begins to seem empty. Back in the

Fifties, Patti Page asked our parents the musical question, "Is that all there is?"

Now we're asking ourselves the same thing.

Starting back in college, I wanted to achieve self-actualization. So I studied people who *seemed* to have it. Copying them, I hit the money trail. In short order, I acquired recognition, income, and power. I was bulletproof on financial security.

I had enough trappings to feed my ego and proclaim I was a player, but I did *not* achieve self-actualization.

Why? I was parked on the "career" level—the middle zone where most successful people get stuck. I wasn't alone. Maslow said only 2 percent of people will ever reach the state of self-actualization.

At a certain point, I realized that I wasn't self-actualized because my golf score was dropping, or I was traveling to resorts. At some point, I began to realize that maybe my successes were actually just stepping stones so I could make a *real* contribution later on.

In the 1970s, Maslow's original five-level pyramid was expanded. The new top floor is "transcendence needs." This altruistic goal of motivating and guiding fellow climbers is actually three levels above "self-actualization."

Simply put, Level Eight means helping *others* achieve self-actualization.

One man who embodies Level Eight, "transcendence," is my friend and mentor, Peter Thomas. At age 80, Thomas is vibrant, energetic, and contributing at an international level. "I want to use my skills, network, and influence to make the world a better place."

Born in 1938, Thomas is an entrepreneur, investor, author, and philanthropist. There isn't room to list his accomplishments, but among them, Thomas founded Century 21 Real Estate in Canada. He served as its chairman until selling his rights in 1987, when the company had $9 billion in annual sales and employed over 8,000 sales representatives with 450 franchises.

In 2000, Thomas moved to Scottsdale, Arizona, and led the development of the Four Seasons Resort and Hotel, among other activities. Always eager to share his insights, Thomas is actively involved in Young Presidents' Organization (YPO) and was a founding member of the Entrepreneurs' Organization (EO).

At the age of 73, Thomas founded Thomas Franchise Solutions (TFS), a private equity firm that develops businesses in North America with franchising as their expansion strategy. Two years later, TFS invested in "Dogtopia," a rapidly growing dog boarding and grooming franchise.

Thomas unabashedly shares the keys to his success: "My values, my visualization, my inspiration, and the ability to reflect back. But values are the key thing. When you know what your values are, you can always fall back on them. My key values are health, happiness, freedom, and integrity. I make sure nothing conflicts with any of those."

To share his experience and philosophy of values-based living and leadership with others, Thomas founded the nonprofit organization LifePilot (*lifepilot.org*). Thomas sums up his formula, "When your values are clear, your decisions become easier."

In your second-half work life, "looking for a job" is better thought of as "searching for significance." After 50, it's especially important that you don't settle for an unfulfilling occupation or just chase after money. This is your big chance to make your mark, to do the right thing for the right reasons.

## Don't Retire. Yes, that's what I said.

By 2050, there will be 84 million Americans over 65 years old. That's more people than Greece, Ireland, Norway, Switzerland, Belgium, Sweden, Hungary, Finland, Austria, Denmark, and Israel *combined*. Can you imagine if they all hit the golf course at once?

A survey ("Work in Retirement: Myths and Motivations") published in 2014 by Merrill Lynch and *Age Wave* said three-quarters of Americans age 50 and over want to work in their retirement. New research indicates half of all Boomers expect to work at least part-time for their *entire life*.

The hard-driving work ethic of this huge generation born between 1946 and 1964 has implications. There are two main reasons why Boomers are digging in their heels and declining to step out of the workforce:

- By choice. As Boomers, we're wired to work. As I said earlier, our Greatest Generation parents taught us the way to get ahead was blood, sweat, and tears. Our "live to work" mentality won't allow us to sit around and play checkers.

- By necessity. As a group, many of us saved too little, spent too much, and took on mountains of personal debt. Then 2008 happened. When the recession hit, older Boomers on the cusp of retirement age opted to keep working.

I advocate that second-halfers stay productive to have a positive impact on society, but I'm not naïve. I understand some will opt to continue working for less altruistic motives. Whatever the reason, older Americans are *delaying* voluntary retirement in record numbers.

In fact, more Americans 65 and older are working now than at any time since the turn of the century. That's according to Pew Research Center. They say about 1 in 5 in that bracket are working full-time or part-time. But that's only a hint of what's coming.

The Bureau of Labor Statistics predicts 32 percent of Americans 65 to 74 will still be working in 2022. If you add in the booming underground economy, it's probably exceeding that already.

## Don't Live in Fear.

I'm optimistic. I'm an abundance thinker.

I believe there will always be plenty of good work and open doors for second-halfers. But I think it's fair to say the classic retirement dream has been tarnished by fear—the market bubble may burst, terrorists may destabilize the economy, inflation may devalue our savings; name your own boogeyman.

While economic uncertainty is definitely a factor for some, research shows many of the 78 million or so Baby Boomers see staying in the workforce as a healthy way to stay active and productive.

Because today's older workers are well-educated and highly motivated, they have more options to keep working than previous generations of seniors did—suggesting that their labor-force footprint will keep growing.

Okay, so an entire chunk of my generation may not retire. Is that bad? If you think linear, it could pose problems. But if you think exponentially, these legions of older workers can be a huge windfall for our country as a whole.

An article in *The Economist* (slyly titled, "A Billion Shades of Gray") predicts, "The trend will benefit not just fortunate oldies, but society as a whole…Government budgets will be in better shape as high earners pay taxes longer."

Don Lee of the *Los Angeles Times* adds, "Better educated, older workers…help the country's precarious fiscal situation; by working, they're paying Social Security and other taxes rather than drawing public retirement and Medicare funds."

*The Economist* sums it up, "Age should no longer determine the appropriate end of a working life."

## Don't Retire, Re-Fire.

Let's be honest. Some are nervous that our nation can't afford being top heavy with aging Boomers. They're worried about who'll pick up the tab for Social Security and other age-related expenses.

It's a fair question.

Here's my short answer. By not retiring, Boomers won't be the *problem*, they'll be the *solution*. By seeing big problems as big opportunities, they'll use exponential technologies to address local and global issues that are waiting to be solved by seasoned entrepreneurs.

I agree with my friend, Peter Diamandis, that due to exponentially growing technologies, we'll soon be able to meet and exceed the basic needs of every man, woman, and child on earth. Diamandis says, "For the first time in history, our capabilities have begun to catch up to our ambitions."

Technology is advancing to the point where dreams like wiping out preventable diseases and supplying safe water for all populations will become a reality. In his watershed book, *Abundance: The Future Is Better Than You Think*, Peter outlines three powerful forces that are lining up to improve life on earth:

- **The rise of the bottom billion.** Due largely to the communication revolution, the world's poorest have recently begun plugging into the global economy, both as consumers and producers of goods.

- **The rise of tech philanthropists.** A new breed of donors is applying their immense wealth to the developing world. Tech entrepreneurs account for roughly half of all donations made by the top fifty US philanthropists.

3. **The rise of do-it-yourself innovation.** Small organizations and even individuals are now able to make huge contributions,

even in the most advanced tech domains (computing, biotechnology, and space travel).

The third force is where *you* come in!

Diamandis's purpose is to inspire people of any age to enter the fray with their own contributions toward abundance.

Today, "novices"—from teenagers to octogenarians—astonish the "experts" with their creativity. And if you've gained special skills in the course of your career, so much the better. You can join one of the numerous open-source innovation projects available online, raise funds on Kickstarter, or apply for one of the many incentivized technological prizes.

So, be the early adopter, the outsider, the risk-taker, regardless of your age. March to a different drummer. Shock the naysayers by doing something remarkable.

## Our Most Valuable Resource.

America's relatively new idea of retirement traditionally meant withdrawal from productive employment. Yet throughout history, people have always found meaning and motivation by doing fulfilling work—at any age. Going back to that historic model, Boomers are extending their working lives and using their wisdom, training, and experience to heat up our economy.

Author Chris Farrell shares my vision for a positive outcome. "If society taps into the abilities and knowledge of those Boomers eager to embrace their unretirement, employers will benefit, society will be richer, and the funding shortfalls of old-age entitlements much easier to solve."

Farrell is author of *Unretirement: How Baby Boomers Are Changing the Way We Think About Work, Community, and the Good Life*. To those worried about Boomers being a drag on the economy, he says, "A series of broad, mutually reinforcing changes in the US economy and society are turning an aging population into more of an economic asset than ever before. Boomers are well-educated and they're healthier than previous generations. An information and services dominated economy is easing the transition to longer work lives."

I view the rise of older workers as a huge bonus for strained state and federal budgets—this group of high-earners will help fill the tax coffers and stimulate the economy. On top of that, motivated seniors will demonstrate and transfer good work ethics and values to younger workers.

A Gallup series called, "Many Baby Boomers Reluctant to Retire" challenges CEOs: "It is important that organizations build workplaces with outstanding managers who leverage the experience of older workers by positioning them to do what they do best—listening to their insights and opinions, and continuing to develop their talents into strengths."

One of the most frustrating things I see as an advisor is how companies waste productivity opportunities by underutilizing their older workforce. By using the wrong retirement model, they fail to leverage an age group that is fundamentally self-directed and willing to work on a modified schedule with lower benefits.

Tapping into this valuable resource can be a huge return on investment—moving from two times to ten times ROI if properly managed. The standard "20-and-out" or "30-and-out" retirement model was instituted with good intentions, but wasting such proven talent is a disservice to the company and the departing worker.

Why would any company let seasoned, self-managed employees walk out the door and go play bingo somewhere? Experienced workers have a track record of skills and integrity that are hit-and-miss with newly hired employees. It makes more sense for the company to renegotiate a package with a flexible work schedule so senior workers can have more time off and more freedom (which they've earned). At the same time, they'd be leveraging those unique pearls of wisdom in a more effective and targeted manner.

Chris Farrell agrees. "If an organization wants innovation to flourish, the conversation needs to change from severance packages to retention bonuses."

Employers often face frustration when trying to find younger workers whose vision and values align with theirs. It's been said you can teach *skills* but you can't teach *values*. So you have to locate candidates who already have your company values and partner with them. Unfortunately, finding the HR needle in the haystack is getting harder with each passing year.

"Today's young generation is simply *not* anchored to the bedrock ethical values of honesty, respect for others, personal responsibility, and civic duty," says Los Angeles law professor Michael Josephson. He blames a "me-first" value system.

That's the beauty of the mature workforce. They come preloaded with the "values software" employers want most—they're hardworking, highly motivated, and self-managing. What Boomers know cannot be taught from books or seminars. It comes from on-the-job experience and from emulating parents who survived tough times.

Julius Caesar said it first, "Experience is the teacher of all things."

## A Real-Life Win-Win.

Recently, a company I work with was going to retire their CFO. What happened instead is evidence of a trend that is repurposing a potent workforce. At the time, he was earning over $450,000 a year. In his position, he managed a whole plethora of performance criteria. I suggested they retain him on a modified basis. The company agreed. They divided up his responsibilities among three up-and-coming leaders. He now works on a contract basis, supporting and mentoring this trio of younger employees. His experience, trustworthiness, and depth of knowledge make him an ideal candidate for this kind of arrangement.

The company is happy because they can access his unique skills for 25 percent of his former rate. He is happy because he is contributing value in his area of unique ability—and adding to his second-half income stream.

Plus, he now has time for recreational pursuits, grandkids, and other interests. Recycling is good. Repurposing is better.

Instead of tossing "used" workers out (or relegating them to a life of delivering pizzas or greeting shoppers), let's repurpose older employees and tap into their wisdom and experience in a win-win scenario. Whether they're on flextime or part-time, employers can have access to what made them great workers in the first place—skill, character, and reliability.

## LEAVE A LEGACY

It used to be that once an employee left a company, it didn't want them back. Yet, these days, a growing trend in recruiting is known as "boomerang employees." Companies are now embracing workers who quit and then come back. If you have left your organization without burning any bridges, you may find your former employer receptive to hiring you, and often for part-time hours. It's much easier and less expensive for a company to bring back someone who is already familiar with how the place works. The boomerang phenomenon makes the company look good, too. It shows other potential hires how much better the company is to an employee who has experienced work with other companies, yet made the choice to come back. Sharing this news through social media or company newsletters can create great PR for an organization.

So, rather than wondering where in the world you might work, you might want to consult your contacts app for phone numbers you once knew very well.

# Work Part Time: At Your Old Job or a New One.

Late-night talk host, Arsenio Hall, used to begin his CBS show with the catchphrase, "Let's get busy!" My twist on his trademark is, "Let's *stay* busy!" My goal for you is to *stay* creative, *stay* productive, and *stay* financially self-sustaining throughout your senior years.

Okay, so a huge block of Boomers will stay in the workforce. The question is where? Hint: it won't necessarily be nine-to-five in the corner office, production facility, retail environment, or other traditional venue.

A large segment of this talented generation will be doing *meaningful* work, operating *off-site* from anywhere they choose, on schedules of their *own making*. If you're a Boomer, the employment landscape is changing for the better—if you're flexible, teachable, and willing to kiss the old stereotypes goodbye.

Chris Farrell likes this flexibility. "For some, their encore job may be full-time, but for the majority their next act is likely to embrace the flexibility that comes from part-time jobs, contract work and temp employment. Older workers are carrying their existing skills into new settings."

A teacher might move from a high school to teaching ESL classes in the evenings. A physician's assistant might shift from a large hospital to a community clinic. An attorney might go from a big practice to focusing on family law part-time. A CPA could leave his firm and teach finance to fledgling entrepreneurs.

When Dolly Parton wrote her hit song "9 to 5" back in 1980, most Americans could relate. But in the almost four decades since that tune debuted, we've been steadily moving away from a 40-hour, Monday-through-Friday workweek toward a balancing act called "work-life integration."

This organic blending of *career demands* and *personal life* will be absolutely the norm for Boomers going forward.

Far-fetched? Thanks to the exponential growth of digital communication, many US workers are *already* practicing work-life integration. For better or worse, certain employees are already living the new "always-on" corporate lifestyle.

There are big benefits, but there's also a downside. With today's 24/7 access, we can experience what media theorist Douglas Rushkoff calls "present shock." In his book, *Present Shock: When Everything Happens Now,* Rushkoff writes, "We live in a continuous, always-on NOW and lose our sense of long-term narrative and direction." He suggests it's so easy to be overwhelmed by an always-on reality that our human bodies and minds can never truly catch up. If that happens, expect frustration, burnout, and adrenaline overload.

## LEAVE A LEGACY

They have been called, "See you next year workers." Planned seasonal work is increasingly popular, particularly with "retired" Boomers. They fill positions at places that have to build up their staff for peak times of year, such as national parks, ski mountain resorts, or amusement parks. These seniors routinely work a season and then return the following one. Snowbirds also fall into this category. Working at one of the country's many national parks, monuments and historic sites in particular is a great option for retirees. Nearly a third of the national park workforce is over the age of 50. The National Park Service relies on thousands of seasonal employees for jobs such as giving ranger talks about history and nature, manning the entry gates, and shuttling employees from housing to work. And that housing often is a perk that comes with the job. If you don't want to work full-time, and if you like meeting people, why not enjoy the great outdoors?

So keep your balance. And your boundaries.

More and more, fixed-schedule employment is being replaced by flex-time options. And that's good for post-retirement age workers. We'll call our own shots. Pick our own schedules. Exponential tech will allow seasoned workers to have new job options—including multiple 1099 employers, virtual businesses, multinational clientele, total flex-time, and roles we haven't dreamed of yet.

It's how I work and it's where the world is headed.

## Be Your Own Boss.

You are the right age to start a business. A full third of new business start-ups are by folks over 50, as more and more Baby Boomers say goodbye to first-season careers.

"The rise of the 'retire-preneur' does more than give the aging population something to pass the time; it's allowing them to contribute to the economy by creating a rich ecosystem of knowledge and support for entrepreneurs across the board." That's from a *Forbes* article, "Why Boomers Are Ditching Retirement to Start Their Own Business." Author Brian Scudamore adds, "By using their life's experience to lead their own businesses, this cohort is passing their wisdom on to the next generation. Their second careers are an opportunity to advise and coach business leaders of tomorrow."

Another plus is that mature workers can often support more than one company at a time as consultants or independent contractors. In my case, I advise and coach twelve different companies. This helps *me* obviously, but each client also benefits from what I learn by observing best practices (and mistakes) of a dozen successful organizations! And by spreading my income stream across multiple sources, I am insulated from a possible downward shift in any one of them. That's a good business model for workers of any age.

That's exciting. But use caution. With Boomers, there's always a propensity for burnout. Always the urge to cross the line between "self-regulating" and "overworking." Most of us already do work emails and video conferencing from home. Nights, weekends, vacations; we're never off the grid. It's invasive. And it's only going to get worse. As you transition to part-time or off-site, be diligent not to chuck your privacy by granting an unhealthy level of round-the-clock access.

Think back to the advent of office gear like fax machines and word processors. These vintage breakthroughs *did* make certain tasks faster, but any time we gained was filled up with…that's right—more work.

Each new labor-saving device promises leisure. But after decades of automation, workloads and stress levels keep going up. In our second-half work life, we'll need to build in rejuvenation time for recreation, exercise, education, family, and rest.

―――――――

You may find opportunity in *unexpected*, yet transferrable skills.

What does laundry have to do with award-winning lemon pie?

Ask Andy Hilton of Florida who had a successful 40-year career managing commercial laundry operations. When his wife became ill, he started baking on the weekends as a creative activity he and his wife could enjoy at home. He brought the homemade pies and cakes to his employees and clients. Soon, he was getting calls with requests. The baking was relaxing and he loved the smiles and excitement of his weekend customers. In his free time, he studied baking techniques. He began adding some large-scale equipment to his kitchen. At the age of 55, Andy gave up the late-night emergency phone calls that were all too common in laundry work to become a full-time baker.

There is a logic to this transition. Andy's experience working with laundry chemical formulas translated seamlessly into a keen understanding of bakery chemistry. You may have seen him on Florida TV affiliates demonstrating his "formulas" or recently on the Food Channel as the winner in the professional category of the National Pie Championship.

# Boom or Bust.

A billion people over 65. In our lifetime. That's an unimaginable number. It took all of human history up to 1804 for the world population to reach a billion!

Incidentally, population is a perfect example of exponential growth. The year 1804 marked the first billion. But it only took 123 years to reach the next billion in 1927. After that, the rate really accelerated—three billion in 1959, four billion in 1974, five billion in 1987, six billion in 1999, and now 7.6 billion.

In case you're wondering, we're adding a billion more every 12 years.

Now imagine a billion senior citizens alive at one time. According to the "Billion Shades of Gray" study, it's coming soon. "Over the next 20 years, the global population of those aged 65 or over will almost double, from 600 million to 1.1 billion."

As we said earlier, you can view the population boom as a fiscal disaster or an economic godsend. *Prepared* people over 50 will be ready to serve the emerging markets with new products, services, and technologies. *Unprepared* people will be caught off guard and miss one of the best business opportunities in history.

And that's equally true for everyone from executives to welders to nurses.

# The Trouble with Retiring.

As I've shown, the modern American concept of retirement is out of whack. Unfortunately, a lot of people in my age group didn't get the memo. Like me, they grew up hearing that life is 100 percent work until you reach a magic birthday, and then it's 100 percent leisure until you die. Friends, family, and investment gurus tell us the right strategy for our last 20 to 30 years is to shift from working hard to doing virtually nothing.

But guess what? A lot of Boomers aren't buying it anymore. As I talk to people around the country, they're telling me the whole concept makes them uneasy. They are fit, active, and productive, and they can't see why on earth they should totally stop working. They're skeptical about retiring and rightly so.

They want to change the *way* they work, and the *amount* they work, but they definitely want to keep earning and contributing to society. They want to maintain some level of employment or entrepreneurial endeavor combined with more free time for sport fishing, skiing, traveling, whatever. They're longing for a hybrid alternative to the dead end of traditional retirement.

Whether they can articulate it or not, I get the sense they're looking *to replace retirement with intentional living.* And I run into them all the time.

I recently got a ride from an older limo driver with a fantastic attitude. He told me he was born in Cuba and had six kids. He worked hard, made good money, and was able to retire at age 57. Then he shared a startling confession—after just three months of leisure, he was bored stiff. Going crazy. So he bought a Lincoln Town Car and started a new career as his own boss. Now he works when he wants and where he wants. He has total freedom to take days (or weeks) off to enjoy his family. He is excited, independent, and adding value to society.

He's just one example of millions operating similar hybrid work-life situations.

I think this ambitious group is on the right track.

---

*"Life is like a bicycle. You don't fall off unless you stop pedaling."*

—CLAUDE PEPPER

# THREE DRIVERS TO SECOND-HALF SUCCESS

## ACHIEVING NEW LEVELS OF MEANING, PURPOSE, AND IMPACT

"*Growth is the only evidence of life. The opposite is true, too. Stagnation is the first step to your grave.*"

—JOHN O'LEARY

"*The heart of human excellence often begins to beat when you discover a pursuit that absorbs you, frees you, challenges you, or gives you a sense of meaning, joy, or passion.*"

—TERRY ORLICK

# Three Opportunities with Big ROI.

You and I are at a unique point in our lives. Old enough to look backward and see our victories and defeats. Young enough to look forward and profit from everything we've learned. That's a huge advantage. Science says the human body is designed to last twelve decades. Let's shoot for a big chunk of that. And not as an enfeebled, doddering oldster, but as a vibrant contributor.

Your second half can be invigorated and energized by living out one or more of three opportunities I now present to you. You can do all three at once, but will benefit most by focusing your energy on one, and enjoying the other two as additional fuel. They are:

1. **Pursue Professional Mastery**

2. **Revive a Dream**

3. **Improve Your World**

All three create value, all three give energy. All three will make the second half of your life better than the first.

Why does any of this matter? Why not just kick back and drift? In his book, *On Fire*, John O' Leary says if you're not on fire for something, you're wasting your life. And he should know. As a boy, O'Leary nearly died in a devastating house fire, suffering burns on 100 percent of his body. His hard-fought recovery took years—and an almost unimaginable amount of inner strength. The ordeal taught him life lessons he now shares worldwide. To anyone facing obstacles or uncertainties, he counsels, "You can't always choose the path you walk in life, but you can always choose the manner in which you walk it."

That's good advice for those of us at or near retirement age—after all, we face a daunting array of opportunities...*and* choices. O'Leary says, "Living on fire is a choice. A choice we commit to and choose daily." He dares us to choose the path (different for each of us) that will most transform our life from success to significance—and see how many lives we can positively impact along the way.

With that goal in mind, let's explore each of our three opportunities.

1. Pursue Professional Mastery.

Unlike previous generations, the majority of Baby Boomers intend to keep working after they hit retirement age. I applaud that decision. At this stage of life, I encourage you to keep working—but in a new way for a new reason.

Do what you enjoy. Do what brings you energy. And use your wealth of experience to redefine what success means.

In our first-half careers, many of us pursued success as identified by matrixes like income, achievements, and getting to the top. That's fine. That kind of drive got the economy roaring and gave Boomers an amazing lifestyle. But there's a downside. John O'Leary says, "When you chase success, your spark burns out quickly. When you do something of significance, the spark jumps to life, spreads to others, and burns brightly long after you are gone."

Our youth and lack of life experience often required that we learn and apply knowledge and energy in pursuits that provided security and frequently stroked our ego. As O'Leary stated, it gave us a "spark" of energy but didn't necessarily provide sustained energy and passion. The opportunity for us *now* is to reflect on those valuable experiences from the past to define (or in many cases simply refine) specific areas of expertise where you also gain energy.

That's the difference between work that brings the traditional trappings of success and work that produces lasting significance—*and* leaves a legacy.

The work I'm advocating for you is about using your unique contribution and creativity, coupled with flexibility, and opting out of the mainstream. It's about feeling empowered, fulfilled, and valuable.

Mastery is defined as a comprehensive knowledge or skill in a subject or accomplishment. My definition of professional mastery is narrowing down your scope to include only those specific items that give you consistent energy and a deep sense of contribution to humanity.

I am assuming that during your career stage you took on greater levels of responsibility and authority as you went along, and were in turn rewarded financially for it. In this *next* stage, I am encouraging you to narrow your focus to those few things that you never tire of learning about, exploring, and discussing. I suggest you give yourself permission to go much deeper into your area of unique contribution. The payoff of this approach is you will likely earn just as much or more money for your unique contribution—while putting in less effort!

In fact, you may find yourself in a similar situation to me, where you reflect with gratitude, "I can't believe I get paid for doing this." Some of us are blessed to be in that situation earlier in our careers, but I think it's less than 20 percent. Early in my career, I was fortunate to be invited to lead a small business as president coupled with the capital to have an equity stake. At that time, I assumed that if I could be the CEO, it would be the pinnacle of my career. However, I found many aspects of the role did not give me energy and in fact were quite stressful. Yet, there were some elements that did give me energy. As I continued my journey (coupled with my enjoyment in continuous learning), I discovered my unique contribution and how to focus that energy. In parallel, I also learned to surround myself with others whose unique contribution helped leverage my skills and gave us a collective outcome greater than the individual parts.

Perhaps you'll start a business of your own—some assert there are more people *over* 50 than *under* 50 doing that today. Or, perhaps, you'll come back to your current employer, but as a 1099 employee. Lots of talented people work for more than one corporation, contributing value and doing only what they enjoy most and have a unique ability for. And they do it when and where they choose.

That's what I do.

Over the years, I've weeded out work activities in finance and operations. Truthfully, I didn't enjoy doing them much and they drained my energy. Streamlining my "second-half work" allows me to focus almost exclusively on what I do best and enjoy most—developing relationships, coaching and facilitating teams, and investing significant time and money in growing and sharpening my skills. At the same time, I can work fewer hours, add more value, and still receive excellent compensation for my efforts.

30 years ago, management thinker, Charles Handy, foresaw a shift away from the traditional nine-to-five, Monday through Friday workplace. In fact, he actually envisioned much of the work-life balance I currently recommend. In his 1989 book, *The Age of Unreason*, Handy predicted that in the future (now!), people would only spend half their working hours in formal employment environments. They'd spend the other half doing what he dubbed "portfolio work"—a blend of part-time jobs, consulting work, and temporary work for multiple employers.

Sound good? Professional mastery looks different for each individual, but think hard about maximizing your impact while freeing yourself from doing whatever you consider burdensome and energy draining.

I'm honored to have someone who's achieved professional mastery and epitomizes its benefits within my own circle of friends.

Dave Dudon, for example, didn't fall into the retirement trap. At age 55, he sold the family business. Although he could have very easily retired, he chose not to. "I would've had to adjust my lifestyle and I didn't want to. But more importantly, I enjoy working and was excited by the opportunity to pursue my passion." Today, Dudon is experiencing the best years of his life, working only with clients he enjoys, on a schedule of his own design. "I feel a little guilty about being paid for the work I do. Not that it doesn't have value, but because I enjoy it so much."

How long will Dave stay at it? He's currently sixty-nine, and has his sights set on age 80 as the time to reassess his career—or rather, his calling. "If I can still provide value and continue to enjoy my vocation as much as I do today, I will continue working indefinitely." In addition to his business consulting work, Dave teaches Family Business at the University of Dayton, a pursuit he enjoys fully as much as his coaching and advising. He even got his wife, Mary Anne, into the business. Initially, they became co-facilitators for a series of twelve business topics as an adjunct to his coaching/advising with The CEO Advantage process. Turns out they enjoyed working and spending time together so much that she joined him in his client strategic planning sessions. And she's great at it! Recently, Dave had to step away from a lunch meeting with clients. When he returned, the leadership team exclaimed, "Why'd you bother coming back? Mary Anne had it handled."

It's not all work for Dave and Mary Anne; they love spending time with their three daughters and eight grandchildren. Dave's also an avid golfer and enjoys playing at his primary club in Dayton as well as at their second home in Florida.

Dave Dudon really reflects all three of the lifestyle options. He continues to pursue a level of professional mastery in driving increased value to his clients, he pursues an artistic expression in his teaching, and finally, he volunteers on the Alzheimer's Association Board, serving the community in an area he has deep affinity with.

Dave's life is rich and purposeful. Isn't that better than retirement? As you consider your second half, I invite you to be this new kind of self-actualized person. The kind who can't wait to wake up each day and make a difference. Many years ago, Steve Jobs found his key to professional mastery: "The only way to do great work is to love what you do. If you haven't found it yet, keep looking, and don't settle. As with all matters of the heart, you'll know when you find it."

2. Revive a Dream.

In January 1895, American author Henry James debuted a play on the London stage. It was a total disaster and a financial failure.

James was 53 years old at the time. Friends and family urged him to quit and retire. He was wealthy and respected, with guaranteed income. Well-wishers told him to sit back and enjoy the success of his earlier novels, like *Washington Square* and *Portrait of a Lady*.

Refusing to bow out, James redoubled his efforts. "Large and full and high the future still opens. It is now indeed that I may do the work of my life."

In the years to follow, James wrote numerous masterpieces including, *The Turn of the Screw*—arguably his greatest work. Henry James perpetually saw his future as "large and full and high." For anyone approaching (or exceeding) middle age, that's great advice. Repeated and acted upon, it can change our entire outlook.

As James worked through his old age, he told friends that he was becoming *more* creative and *more* willing to take risks than in his youth.

What does this story tell you? It's time to reignite your passion.

A wonderful option in the second half is reviving that dream. You know, the one you left behind to get a *real job*. You now have more time, more wisdom, and a lifetime of experiences to draw from and express. The first-half demands of building a career and raising a family required millions of talented Baby Boomers to put their creative dreams on hold.

Now that you have greater control of your schedule, indulge yourself in the arts, sciences, and athletics.

If you're visually inclined, get those oil paints out of the closet. Grab a sketchbook and head outdoors. Try a class in graphic design or letterpress. Take that photography class you've been putting off. Join the ranks of over-fifty artisans who are bringing beauty to society.

We often think of artists as young and brash. But the man called "England's most important painter" busted that myth. Extraordinarily inventive, J. M. W. Turner produced his most important and famous pictures after the age of sixty. Pioneering radically new techniques, Turner's later works dumbfounded his contemporaries and rattled critics.

Pablo Picasso was another rebel who never slowed down. He created 300 sculptures, 13,500 paintings, 34,000 book illustrations, and 100,000 prints. Remarkably, six of his top ten works were composed after age 50. This icon worked at genius levels until he died during a dinner party at 99 years old.

Maybe you're a writer or a poet. If so, massage that gift and share it with the world. Self-publish a book on your favorite subject. Submit short stories to local publications. Start a blog. Collect oral histories. Write a novel. Join a writers' group.

You can call upon the wisdom you have gained from your career. Peter Drucker was one of the most influential thinkers on management theory and practice. He consulted IBM, GE, Procter & Gamble, Intel, and several US presidents. *Business Week* called him, "the man who invented management." In all, Drucker wrote 39 books in his career. And here's the wild part—he wrote two-thirds of them after age 65 (they're considered his best). Instead of retiring, he worked joyfully until he died just short of his 96 birthday.

## LEAVE A LEGACY

Who knows what will become of your efforts? For instance, having a bestseller is rare for a first-time author. It's even rarer when the author's a white-haired, retired schoolteacher. Yet, *Angela's Ashes*, Frank McCourt's tale of growing up in grinding poverty in the slums of Ireland, sold over four million copies. At age sixty-six, McCourt told *The New York Times*, "I'm a late bloomer" shortly after the publication of his book in 1996.

But the late bloomer wasn't finished. In 2005, he released *Teacher Man* at age 75 to international acclaim and a demanding schedule of tours and talk shows.

McCourt's late-in-life literary career propelled him from obscurity to fame and fortune. In *Teacher Man*, he gave advice that applies to any of us in our second half: "Find what you love and do it. That's what it boils down to."

I wouldn't dare put myself in the same category as these authors, but I'll tell you a little about how I came to love writing. After choosing to pursue it, I made two very helpful decisions. The first was finding a writing partner like Karl Nilsson. I find it's always easier to take on a new task or venture with the assistance of someone who has more experience in a given field. The second and equally important decision was scheduling time each morning to actually write. In essence, I was fulfilling the two commitments: **Be Inspired** (to become a writer) and **Manage Your Energy** (schedule time to write daily).

The creative possibilities hardly stop there, however. Did you dream of being a naturalist? Michigan trains volunteers to be citizen-scientists who monitor water quality in our many freshwater lakes. Archaeologists accept hardworking volunteers at home and abroad. Who didn't think about becoming a golf pro? Teach youth at a public course. My wife's childhood dream was to be a jazz singer. She found her stage by turning her marketing career into a gig teaching college students. Is empathy your skill? Many social workers, psychologists, and counselors get certified later in life. Their life experiences make them excellent advisers.

Maybe you like to build things. Dust off that workshop and get busy. *Xprize.com* has projects just waiting for innovative solutions that will massively impact lives, so does Habitat for Humanity. Combine your childhood dreams and the skills you developed over decades. Apply your experience in finance, leadership, logistics, sales, or technology. Do you love the outdoors? Manage a campground. Organize the community garden.

Whatever your bottled-up passion, go from "pause" to "play" and you'll be doing yourself and your family a service.

## Choices Abound. Opportunities are endless.

If you love music, unpack that guitar. Tune up that piano. Enroll in lessons, join a group, or have a jam session. If you played an instrument in high school or college, you'll find enormous joy and energy in picking it back up.

A local businessman who did just that still remembers his biggest inspiration.

## An Encore Worth Pursuing.

On February 9, 1964, 73 million people gathered around their televisions to watch The Beatles' first live performance on the *Ed Sullivan Show*. One of those viewers was 11-year-old Terry Altman.

It made a huge impression on the musically inclined boy. The very next day he asked a friend at school to show him how to play guitar. Within 24 hours of the broadcast, Terry began teaching himself how to pick and strum, with a dream of someday being a rock star. Without ever taking a formal lesson, Altman quickly became accomplished on guitar and piano. While in high school, he started several rock bands. Entering college, he transitioned to folk rock. Influenced by the likes of Bob Dylan, he was soon playing acoustic performances around the Washington University campus and St. Louis area. Later, he organized what he calls "a Grateful Dead cover band." In 1975, he teamed up with an audio engineer to form a production company. It wasn't long before he released his own album, "Crosswalk." A mix of progressive rock, jazz, and deeply personal lyrics, every song was written by the budding composer.

Then life took a giant twist. Altman felt called to the ministry and entered Bible college in Tulsa. He was soon recruited to play guitar for a national ministry that toured the country. After that, he went on to found and direct a ministry-training institute in Metro Detroit. Next up, Altman planted a brand-new church in the Detroit suburbs. Six years later, he was recruited again—this time by a group doing financial consulting for nonprofit organizations. As a former pastor, Terry excelled at this and began doing tax advising and retirement planning for ministers. Setting his music aside, Terry pursued higher levels of training in his new field and gained numerous credentials, including certified financial planner. With hard work and long hours, he focused on his career and education.

In 2001, Terry dusted off his musical skills and began a 15-year run as a volunteer musician at a megachurch in Southeast Michigan. Playing keyboards at the weekend services "scratched his musical itch" and allowed him to personally counsel and mentor dozens of other volunteer musicians. All this on top of working 50 hours a week as a busy financial planner!

As Terry's client list grew over the years, he was eventually able to dial down his "day job" hours and get back to playing music gigs around town, both as a soloist and with a duo partner. "Connecting with an audience gave me energy. Playing in front of people lets me know that what I do artistically matters." At age sixty-four, Terry again defied stereotypes by taking master classes from an Italian concert pianist. He says, "Chopin. Beethoven. 50 years after I began playing, I was finally really learning my instrument." History is full of painters, authors, and naturalists who did their finest and best-known work after sixty. As we saw earlier, geniuses like Picasso, Monet, and Wagner worked at a high level well into their old age. If they could do it, so can you. Best of all, you'll be adding your creative energy to a world that needs what you have to offer.

Pick up your dream where you left off or start from scratch. Either way will fill your heart and keep your brain razor sharp. Like the Czech novelist, Franz Kafka said, "Anyone who keeps the ability to see beauty never grows old."

3. Improve Your World.

Capitalism has never been so charitable. From Walmart to TOMS shoes, corporate America is helping to meet local and global needs at a record pace.

Many major corporations are putting social responsibility at the core of their business model. And wisely so. To an increasing number of stockholders, a company's social footprint is just as important as their financial health. In fact, "doing well by doing good" has almost become institutionalized.

As a result, you might be tempted to think the big corporate players have it covered. Or maybe you look around and think the world's problems are so enormous that an individual like you can't make a difference.

Wrong on both counts.

You are absolutely needed, and in my mind, obligated to pitch in.

One of the benefits as we age is that our priorities and perspectives change from "inward" to "outward." This shift manifests with older individuals using their accumulated business acumen and life skills to help others. This urge to be a positive force for change can range from meeting local needs (like tutoring school kids or stocking a food pantry) to tackling international issues (like human trafficking or preventable childhood diseases).

The role of the "little guy" in solving problems cannot be overstated. Lives and communities are improved *one person at a time* through millions of small interactions. John O'Leary encourages us to look for "small" opportunities to improve our world. The kinds of problems we could help solve right in our own backyards. Makes sense. It's easy to feel overwhelmed or become emotionally immobilized by the immense needs. But rather than stalling out, we can begin to focus on smaller opportunities that tend to pass us by. O'Leary says, "Decide today to make your family, your community, your organization, your world, a better place. Pay attention. Ask, 'What more can I do?'"

Did you notice the progression from small to large? Some of you will start by making an impact in your own community. Others will feel compelled to travel across the globe to make a difference.

## LEAVE A LEGACY

Richard Fahey, sixty-nine, a former Peace Corps volunteer in Liberia in the 1960s, returned to visit the country to assess the conditions after years of civil war. Soon after, Fahey retired from his law practice and became a fellow at Harvard University. During the next year, Fahey developed the business model for the Liberian Energy Network, a nonprofit organization. Since the company began, it has provided thousands of solar lights and electricity to homes, businesses, and hospitals across the country.

"Every human life contains a potential; if that potential is not fulfilled, then that life was wasted." Those are the words of Carl Jung, the Swiss psychiatrist credited with inventing analytical psychology. Sigmund Freud's sparring partner was a pioneer in recognizing the positive impact of what he called "oldsters" on society. Jung himself lived to be 85 and continued to publish books until he died in 1961.

Jung said, "Far from being merely candles on a birthday cake, aging can be a time of discovery, growth, development, inner expansion, and enrichment of life."

Considering the productivity of his later years—he called them his most creative—Jung made aging a positive experience. Jung said his later years were "more beautiful than childhood." He was adamant that older people are not finished, but on a great adventure—despite our culture's disdain for the elderly. He encouraged seniors to stay engaged. "The older is called to mentor the younger, and foster creativity in others by following his own creative muse."

As somebody once said, "Wisdom isn't something you can just Google."

You can take more active steps as well. Here is a heartwarming tale of a couple that left their old life behind—and found a richer future in a foreign land.

## To Africa, With Love.

"*Enkosi*" means "thank you" in the Xhosa language. It's a word of gratitude that a Detroit-area couple never expected to hear. But a late-in-life desire to improve the world changed all that.

Bill and Anne Eames enjoyed their comfortable life in the suburbs. Anne was a published author, Bill was a senior project manager for Barton Malow Company. They were surrounded by friends and family, and they were looking forward to the normal perks an upcoming retirement would bring.

Things were humming along until "a new sense of divine purpose" hit them both like a lightning bolt—when they least expected it. Bill and Anne went as volunteers with a church group on a fourteen-day trip to Africa. Something clicked. Without discussing it together, they both individually and independently came to the same conclusion: we will come back here to Africa and make an impact somehow.

They fought the pull for a year. Finally, they made a monumental decision. At age 58, Bill would quit his high-paying job and they would move to Cape Town, South Africa. They would arrive with no income, no job prospects, and no support. They would live on their savings and take it one day at a time.

Bill says, 'I was close to retirement...just one year away from having my 401(k) fully vested. It was a crazy time to make this radical change.'

Anne recalls the upheaval. Step one—sell everything we own. Step two—say goodbye to every friend we had.

Bill adds, 'The hardest part was knowing we would not see our four children and six grandchildren for years.'

'Selling our home. Auctioning off our belongings. It was disruptive,' says Anne. 'But we weren't gloomy. There was a real sense of adventure—a chance to improve one small corner of the world.'

What was their plan? Anne quips, "Not much. I hoped when we got there, I could maybe teach a few folks how to make jewelry. That's it."

Little did they know their "small" idea would grow into a large business—a self-sustaining job creation program for HIV/AIDS sufferers. Called African Hope Crafts, the start-up provided education and employment by training locals to produce hundreds of creative crafts, including jewelry, dolls, knitted items, and accessories. Anne says, "Most of our crafters were unmarried women who were HIV-positive. They had no hope and no way to support themselves."

Over time, distribution and sales grew to include retailers in the Cape Town area and major airports across South Africa. Stores in places like Sweden and Australia started selling our jewelry. The profits paid a living wage to the crafters and we purchased more raw materials for the busy workshop.

"When we started, our crafters lived in dilapidated shacks with leaky tin roofs," notes Anne. "Their hungry children slept on the floor or on wet mattresses. Now, they're dry and warm with electricity and even small refrigerators. Most importantly, they have dignity."

Anne's concept was a success, and strong sales in US churches added to the growth. But Bill knew there was something unique for him to do also. Something directly utilizing job skills he learned in his first-half career in managing construction.

"I was moved by seeing abused, abandoned, and orphaned children. Many street kids had endured horrific circumstances. Creating a safe, nurturing environment for them became my purpose in life." Drawing on his know-how from Barton Malow, Bill constructed three "safe houses" from scratch. Unlike a dormitory, each home was designed to care for at-risk children in a family setting with a loving "house mother" in charge. Separate from African Hope

Crafts, this charity is called African Hope Trust and raises funds internationally to care for vulnerable children.

For ten years, the Eames lived 8,500 miles away, saving lives and changing futures. Today, they're back in the States, but still oversee the continuation of the business and residences—both remotely and by flying over for training new leaders and hands-on mentoring.

Now 72, Bill looks back on leaving everything familiar to go on a humanitarian cause with no guarantee. "It wasn't easy. It cost us dearly in some ways. But I wouldn't trade it for anything."

Maybe, like Bill and Anne, you're wondering if you can find time to do something vitally important. I say you can—but only if you're willing "to make the changes necessary to have a significant second half." That challenge is from Bob Buford's *Half Time: Changing Your Game Plan from Success to Significance.* Buford says older Americans are now "freer to choose what they do than ever before, allowing them to discard the work-related activities that force them to run at full speed all the time."

Improving the world often means leaving our comfort zone. Travelling overseas is no bed of roses. Neither is rescuing at-risk kids. But that's the kind of commitment that creates impact. Bob Buford continues, "For the second half of life to be better than the first, you must make the choice to step outside of the safety of living on autopilot. You must wrestle with who you are, why you believe what you profess to believe about your life, and what you do to provide meaning and structure to your daily activities."

———

This willingness to step outside of our security bubble also describes one of history's greatest authors—and one of history's greatest *volunteers*.

I'm talking about Leo Tolstoy. He was the greatest writer of his time, producing masterpieces, including what is arguably the greatest novel ever written, *War and Peace.* Tolstoy towered above his contemporaries the way Beethoven and Einstein did theirs. And like them, he commanded the world stage until his final days. After his brilliant literary career, the aging superstar dedicated his golden years to transforming society. In his last decade, Tolstoy leveraged his wealth and influence to fight poverty...even shocking his own family by literally giving away a fortune to his causes.

It's fair to say Tolstoy replaced retirement with intentional living as a social reformer, philanthropist, and outspoken critic of the regime. All in his late seventies.

At a life stage when most would enjoy a retreat from working, Tolstoy reinvented himself as a social activist and religious zealot. He transferred his late-blooming ideas about nonviolent resistance directly to his protégé Mahatma Gandhi. Today, the world's largest democracy (India's 1.2 billion people) can trace its independence to ideas forged during Tolstoy's final years.

Before he died in 1910, Russia's exalted novelist found that living a joyous, fulfilling life does not come by retreating from responsibility—but by serving others. Tolstoy said, "Joy can only be real if people look upon their life as a service and have a definite object in life outside themselves and their personal happiness." So drop some nonessential activities. Then roll up your sleeves. What you do behind the scenes may not grab headlines. It may not take you to Africa. It may not train the next Gandhi. But it will improve the world, revitalize your life, and inspire others.

Best of all, you'll create and inspire others to live a legacy of significance and purpose.

Before he was assassinated, Russian revolutionary, Leon Trotsky, once said, "Old age is the most unexpected of all things that can happen to a man." I assume he meant that tongue-in-cheek. Regardless, let's vow *not* to be surprised by old age. Instead, let's surprise the world with what we have to offer.

––––––

At retirement age, we're in the driver's seat. There are no more excuses. Bob Buford sums it up, "The second half is about regaining control of your life—about calling your own shots."

That will involve some discovery (*Where does my Legacy Map lead?*), some intellectual honesty (*What truly gives me lasting energy while making a meaningful contribution?*), and some soul searching (*What do I care most deeply about and what gives purpose to my life?*). When we answer those core questions, we'll map out a path in our life to follow exciting opportunities. And we'll jettison some of the old beliefs and fears that have been holding us back.

Buford says, "Some things will be more important than others; some may need to be ignored altogether. But regardless of what stays and what goes, the point is that we no longer let someone else decide for us. We create capacity for things that matter."

Let's make it our life mission to focus on things that matter.

———

*"Don't ask yourself what the world needs; ask yourself what makes you come alive. And then go do that. Because what the world needs is people who have come alive."*

—HOWARD THURMAN

# STAYING AHEAD
# OF THE GAME

## SECRETS TO STAYING PHYSICALLY
## AND MENTALLY HEALTHY
## EVERY YEAR OF YOUR LIFE

*"A man is not old until regrets replace dreams."*

—JOHN BARRYMORE

*"Happiness is the result of personal effort...you have to
participate relentlessly."*

—ELIZABETH GILBERT

# The Awesome Power of Purpose.

Your life has purpose. Your story is important. Your dreams count. You're on this earth to make an impact.

But how we do define our purpose and push into it?

We met tech entrepreneur Salim Ismail in Section 1. In 2014, he coined the term, Massive Transformative Purpose (MTP) after looking at the one hundred fastest-growing start-ups and identifying common traits. Turns out they all shared a declaration of radical transformation. All were boldly optimistic, some were delightfully outrageous, and all were infused with exponential gusto:

- SpaceX—Enable human exploration and settlement of Mars.

- Google—Organize the world's information and make it universally accessible.

- TED Talks—Ideas worth spreading.

- Amazon—Be the earth's most customer-centric company.

I was inspired. I wondered, *Could an individual create a personal MTP?*

Absolutely! I began developing an MTP that would align my aspirations with the Exponential Age and clarify my purpose for the second half (the best half) of life.

As I worked on it, I followed Ismail's three criteria. An MTP must be: (1) *uniquely yours;* (2) *highly aspirational;* and (3) *aimed at the heart and mind.*

I boiled mine down to six words—**To replace retirement with intentional living.**

As we've seen, this involves revolutionizing traditional retirement paradigms and connecting older Americans into purposeful missions of increasing value. I'm committed to this long term, because an MTP is *aspirational*—always in process, never completed, and always moving toward radical transformation.

That definition should also describe you and me—we're always in process, never completed, and always moving toward our greatest potential. But to reach our second-half goals, we'll need to be *physically healthy* and *mentally sharp*.

## Preventative Maintenance.

Baby Boomers were dubbed the "me generation" by writer Tom Wolfe back in the '70s. And although we did usher in disco and bell-bottoms, we inspired some *good* things also, like jogging and healthier eating. We even started the boom in health clubs (remember Vic Tanny?), workout tapes (remember Buns of Steel?), and fitness gadgets (remember the ThighMaster?).

Today, our generation spends billions on cosmetics, surgeries, and spas to improve our outward appearance. But let's also emulate the *internal* gumption of those who never slowed down.

I grew up watching Detroit Red Wings's star, Gordie Howe become the only NHL player to play in five different decades. At age 52, Howe was the oldest player to ever play in an NHL game.

At 80 years old, Jessica Tandy received the Academy Award for Best Actress *and* the Golden Globe. Henry Fonda copped his Best Actor Oscar at age 76.

Bess Tancrelle celebrated her 102nd birthday by riding a Harley-Davidson. Her helmet is inscribed, "I'm About to Develop an Attitude." Guess this biker was *born to be wild*—in 1907.

I could spend pages listing men and women who've achieved what used to be called impossible for their advanced age—rowing across oceans, climbing mountains, earning advanced degrees, and so much more.

We're not designed to sit around reminiscing about the good old days. Why look back when you can look *ahead*? This holds for even more vigorous exercise. For example, at 99, Teiichi Igarashi climbed Mt. Fuji. Moving into the triple digits, at the ripe old age of 100, Frank Schearer was an active snow and water-skier.

What was Schearer's secret? "I just ski for fun." We can learn a lot about extending healthy living from this centenarian. "I think it has to do with being so active," Shearer said. "I've been active all my life, from one sport to the other—snow skiing in the winter, water-skiing in the summer, hunting, fishing. And, especially in recent years, I've been doing some weight lifting regularly."

So *fun* and *fitness* are two keys.

Speaking of fun, Schearer fell in love and remarried at age 95-five. In November 2010, he blew out 105 candles on his birthday cake.

As Boomers, we were raised to carry our own weight. Our parents told us, "Go out into the world and create value; we're not going to do it for you."

So we learned to be self-reliant. Delivering papers, cutting lawns, selling lemonade—we started young and never took a break. And because it's ingrained in us, we expect it from others.

As a generation, we don't tolerate loafers. Remember the parable of the slothful grasshopper and the industrious ants? When winter comes and there's no food, we don't feel very sorry for the insect who squandered his time, right?

Of course, I'm all in favor of helping the less fortunate. But if someone suffers because of bad choices, it's tougher to be sympathetic. I'm just being honest.

After a lifetime of drinking and smoking, my own mother died of cancer and emphysema in her sixties. She never took care of herself. She was unprepared mentally and physically to fight her illness. Her untimely passing was my incentive to be proactive with good diet, daily exercise, and an active lifestyle.

The importance of preventative maintenance for body and mind was reinforced when I discovered Dr. Charles Eugster. He's known as the "world's fittest nonagenarian" and the world's oldest competitive bodybuilder.

## Beach Bodies at Any Age.

One of the most viewed TED Talks of all time is provocatively titled, "Why Bodybuilding at 93 Is a Great Idea."

The reason for its popularity is the wit and wisdom of a feisty Englishman who seems to have discovered the Fountain of Youth. Minutes after mounting the TED stage in Zurich, Dr. Eugster bowled over his audience with a shocking statistic: 92 percent of Americans over the age of 65 have one or more chronic diseases. In addition, he claims 40 percent of Americans over sixty take at least five medicines per day. While not all illness can be avoided, Dr. Eugster blames inactivity coupled with an epidemic of obesity as the major cause of premature death in folks over 50.

In his sixteen-minute talk, Dr. Eugster outlines three factors that contribute to healthy, successful aging—"Work, diet, and exercise. In that order."

In no uncertain terms, Dr. Eugster proclaims that a main cause of depressed, broken-down, unhealthy seniors is *retirement*. The crowd roars when he proclaims, "Retirement is voluntary or involuntary unemployment for up to 30 years."

The contrarian says retirement causes chronic diseases, mental problems, poor health, and disabilities of all kinds. The antidote is work. "Work is therapeutic, good for health, and an intrinsic part of improving and maintaining good health."

Looking lean and well-muscled, Dr. Eugster claims we can, "rebuild our bodies at any age." He says that getting up in years is not a disaster, but rather a chance to develop dormant talents, create new companies, and start a new (healthier) life.

# The Mind-Body Equation.

In Section 1, we saw how the Exponential Age—driven by information and technology—is affecting energy, networking, and *especially* health care. In his bestseller, *Abundance: The Future Is Better Than You Think,* Peter Diamandis challenged business innovators to utilize the blistering fast progress in areas like synthetic biology, artificial intelligence, and nanotechnology to solve humanity's biggest problems—including disease, aging, and premature death.

As stated earlier, Diamandis is fond of saying, "100 is the new 60." That means if you survive the next fifteen years, you'll see a world where it's as common for people to reach 100 as it is now to reach sixty.

I wondered, *What does that mean to my peers in that age group?*

I focused on Boomers for two reasons. First, I am one. Second, because of what our parents implanted—the notion that we're obligated to take care of ourselves, to serve our community, and to never be a burden on others. That means taking the best possible care of our body and our brain.

The official life span of Americans is 76.4 years for men and 81.2 for women. But science says many of us will reach 100, easily. That's up to 35 percent more life! That's 35 percent more years to live, engage, and contribute to society. Getting 35 percent tacked onto your life span requires a lot of extra planning. (The life-focusing tool called the Legacy Map can help.)

Bottom line? I'm telling my generation two things: It's *our* responsibility (and privilege) to continue contributing value. And it's *our* responsibility to maintain a high level of health and fitness for the next 25 to 40 years.

Anna Quindlen agrees. In *A Short Guide to a Happy Life*, she writes, "You are the only person alive who has sole custody of your life."

## No Pain, No Gain.

Our parents' shining achievement was winning the war and saving democracy. But in an indirect way, their sacrifice was also a *gift* to them. Learning to deal with adversity and hardship strengthened them to live richer, fuller lives. In fact, the one common trait of virtually all super-seniors (people over 90) who perform well in their later years is having faced adversity in their early years.

In order to build a muscle, you must stress it and stretch it. Same for character.

Too much coddling produces a lack of what Dr. Angela Duckworth calls "grit." A psychologist at the University of Pennsylvania, Dr. Duckworth says the biggest predictor of success isn't IQ or even social intelligence. Rather, "It's about having stamina, sticking with your future."

In *Grit: The Power of Passion and Perseverance*, Dr. Duckworth suggests that what drives success is not so much talent, genius, or even luck, but a blend of passion and perseverance that sticks it out no matter what.

Our parents had grit. They grew stronger through hardship. Now it's our turn to discipline ourselves and stay mentally and physically fit—even if it hurts a bit.

Someone said, "Life begins where your comfort zone ends."

In the darkest days of WWII, Winston Churchill said, "If you're going through hell, keep going. Never, never, never give up."

Our parents took his advice and defeated the Axis powers. By defying the negative stereotypes associated with aging, I'm following in their footsteps. I'm extending their legacy by refusing to give up and participate in planned obsolescence.

The number of Americans who turn 65 each year is equal to a country the size of Albania or Ireland. It would be a crime to send them to the junkyard like an old bus with high mileage—or because they let themselves deteriorate physically.

## LEAVE A LEGACY

Folks in Medieval Europe died young, right? Rats, plagues, and high infant mortality kept life expectancy down around 30.

But one man defied the odds and kept on going like the Energizer Bunny.

Alvise Cornaro was a Venetian nobleman born in 1464. Nearly dead at age 40, he went to become a physician. His doctor's advice was, "Cut down your riotous living, stop drinking, eliminate rich food, don't abuse your body, and eat as little as you can."

Cornaro shifted from lavish partying and feasting to a restricted-calorie diet. His book, *La Vita Sobria (Writings on the Sober Life: The Art and Grace of Living Long)* was wildly successful and so was he—he lived to be 102. Brilliant to the end, he published a major book at 95, a guide for "living a long and worthwhile life."

According to contemporaries, Cornaro simply closed his eyes and didn't wake up. No pain or suffering. His mind was clear until the end, without senility or memory loss.

But his remarkable example goes far beyond diet and abstinence. This sixteenth-century thinker believed (like I do) that living longer allows us to nurture and develop what he called those "splendid gifts of intellect and noble qualities of heart" that we often ignore as youth.

He said the best use of God's gifts often "come at the end of life." If that's true, let's be ready—mentally and physically—to leverage them.

# Your Brain Is Built for Lifelong Learning.

"Use it or lose it."

That annoying but true phrase applies to our muscles *and* our brains. Science and medicine now have overwhelming evidence that leading a mentally stimulating life will boost brainpower at any age.

Our lifestyle choices substantially impact the connections in our brain called synapses (we each have over 100 trillion). These microscopic links between nerve cells are involved in memory and learning. And they respond to exercise! Mental *stimulation* increases the size, number, and efficiency of our synapses—resulting in easier, faster learning. Mental *laziness* causes synapses to atrophy—producing slower reaction times and processing of information.

If you'd like to avoid age-related brain decline, keep working, keep learning, keep connecting. In his book, *Aging with Grace*, Dr. David Snowdon describes following a group of 678 Catholic nuns for over 20 years. The results of his long-term "Nun Study" concluded that stimulating intellectual activity and a healthy lifestyle can provide protection from many types of cognitive attrition.

The majority of the sisters were teachers and lifelong learners; studying and sharing knowledge was a common trait. Another characteristic of these remarkable women—ranging in age from 74 to 106—was their overarching dedication to serving others. Sister Schwalbe, one of the convent leaders, told Dr. Snowdon, "Our congregation was founded to work with the poor and powerless."

As a bonus, they live longer and healthier lives. Dr. Snowdon said, "The sisters live dramatically longer lives than their lay counterparts. At one point, in one convent alone, there were seven living centenarians—the sisters called them The Magnificent Seven. Certainly, education and a prudent, healthy lifestyle play an important role. For example, none of the sisters smoke. But I believe that intangibles such as positive life purpose, spirituality, and a supportive community are also significant."

A renowned epidemiologist and expert on Alzheimer's disease, Dr. Snowdon concluded that old age doesn't have to mean an inevitable slide into illness and disability. On the contrary, it can be a time of promise and productivity, bursting with humor, discovery, and intellectual vigor.

In an interview, Dr. Snowdon was asked about his own attitude toward aging. "I'm much more optimistic now than when I was younger. I've known a number of centenarian sisters who are still active and enjoying life. They've made a good old age seem like a real possibility."

I can't begin to understand the beauty and complexity of the human brain. But it seems clear that a "life well-lived" is connected to mental prowess and intellectual longevity. Controllable factors like lifelong learning, positive attitude, and choosing a vocation that benefits others can alter our aging process for the better.

Staying active in the workforce (or in a nun's convent) contributes to what I call the "big four" necessities for keeping our brain sharp, agile, and healthy. They are: *complex mental stimulation, physical fitness, good nutrition,* and *social interaction* with others. Go and do likewise.

For a large dose of mental stimulation, you need look no further than *The New York Times* Sunday edition. It's huge. But even a regular weekday issue contains more information than the average person in seventeenth-century England could access in their entire lifetime!

Science estimates the total of all human knowledge now doubles every ten to fifteen years. And in industries with exponential technologies, information doubles every *five* years. To keep up, we need to be dedicated lifelong learners. And the bonus won't just be a bigger paycheck or sparkling conversations; it will be a *healthier brain.*

Doctors say the sharpest people (of any age) are the ones who give their three-pound organ a regular workout—one that challenges it with rigorous, mind-taxing work. That's why running a charity, mentoring kids, or starting a business is so beneficial to staying mentally "with it."

A lifestyle based on creativity, learning, and engaging with others will increase mental alertness and agility well into our later years, and will perhaps stave off the onset of dementia. Engaging in mind-stretching pursuits reduces our risk of cognitive decline while allowing us to contribute to society.

Legendary UCLA basketball coach, John Wooden, used to put it this way, "If I am through learning, I am through."

## Being All You Can Be.

You've heard the expression, "If only I knew then what I know now."

Well, *this is now*. And the time to create a legacy is *today*. With all that you know at this point in life, with all of your accumulated wisdom, why would you settle for anything less than work that's transcendently satisfying?

One reason we don't strive to "be all we can be" is because we grossly underestimate our own talents and abilities. Millions enjoy *Antiques Roadshow* on PBS. In cities across America, folks bring in old items to be appraised by experts. Often, their flea market treasure is worth less than they paid. But once in a while, fortunes are made.

Likewise, you may have a priceless idea just sitting in your "mental attic" collecting dust. Business and law professor Andrew J. Sherman has written 23 business books. In *Harvesting Intangible Assets,* he educates companies to recognize revenue-producing intellectual properties hiding just below the surface.

His principle applies to individuals as well. We live in a culture of innovation—a new super-flat earth where anybody's homegrown idea can rocket into the mainstream and compete with anyone.

Don't believe it? A single mother of three was frustrated with ordinary mops. Working from home, Joy Mangano developed her first invention, the self-wringing Miracle Mop. With her own life savings and help from friends, she handcrafted 100 units. After selling at local stores on Long Island, she approached QVC. When the cable network allowed Mangano to go on air to sell it herself, she sold 18,000 mops in 20 minutes. Within ten years, her company hit $200 million in sales. Today, she has a total of 100 patents and a net worth of at least $50 million.

All from a homegrown idea. A brainstorm. Your intellectual property has unlimited potential.

If you've got a valuable idea hidden in your mental attic, dust it off and take it to market. Don't keep that idea bottled up. And don't think you missed your window of opportunity. I'll say it again—*your best years are ahead of you.*

In case you're tempted to slack off and coast to the finish line, consider Lillian Weber. She was not a Silicon Valley wonder kid. She never appeared on *Shark Tank*. But she had the late-bloomer idea to use her talents as a seamstress to help others. Her goal was to sew 1,000 dresses for needy kids before she turned 100. When she celebrated her one-hundredth birthday, Weber had surpassed her target by donating 1,051 dresses to Little Dresses for Africa, a nonprofit that helps impoverished girls in forty-seven African countries.

Founder Rachel O'Neill said, "There's no age limit to this. Somebody who is 100 years old and still putting out this quality with such a positive and inspirational message is wonderful. Lives are being saved because of these dresses."

Centenarian Lillian Weber found the secret of happiness and ful-fillment that eludes most people. That kind of intentional living was a subject that intrigued psychologist Abraham Maslow for his entire life.

———

In 1943, Maslow boldly declared, "What a man can be, he must be."

My generation should not settle for "average" when exceptional is so readily available. Maslow challenged us, "If you deliberately plan on being less than you are capable of being, then I warn you that you'll be deeply unhappy for the rest of your life. You will be evading your own capacities, your own possibilities."

Don't we all want to be happy? Fulfilled? Doing what we like? Yes, of course. But it's like they say on the streets, "Everybody wants, but not everybody gets."

## Living at Full Potential in Mind *and* Body.

Maslow said that once our basic survival needs are met, we all aspire to find meaning and purpose in life. He concluded that when our inherent goals match our day-to-day lives, we can be happy. We can be fully alive.

You could say that a self-actualizer is a person who *fully uses their capabilities.*

By that definition, 95-year-old Olga Kotelko certainly qualified. She won hundreds of track and field trophies, even though she didn't enter her first competition until she was 77—an age when most folks trade in their jogging shoes for house slippers. Kotelko took part in 11 events (the hammer throw was her favorite) and traveled the world to compete. Before she passed away in 2014, Olga won 750 gold medals and had broken 30 world records.

Kotelko tapped into this inner motive we all have to express ourselves at the highest level. Sadly, only 2 percent of adults ever find their true self and reach their full potential.

How? We can start by observing what makes this 2 percent so different.

Over years of research, Maslow found one common denominator in people he deemed self-actualized. Without exception, he found they were deeply *devoted to a cause outside themselves*—doing work they felt called to do. Rich or poor, famous or obscure, they all had a *mission to fulfill* or a *problem to be solved*.

When it comes to happiness and life satisfaction, your calling and your job must line up. If you're not there yet, no worries. No guilt. I *guarantee* you are hardwired for growth or you wouldn't be reading this book.

Now it's time to maximize that inherent motivation by finding (or perhaps, creating) a vocation that taps into your overarching life purpose. If you're ready to embrace your unique calling, you may still have one last roadblock. Fortunately, it's fixable.

# Your Plastic, Fantastic Brain.

I used to wonder why some people enjoyed overnight success and then fizzled out. I was puzzled why so many fast starters just faded away.

Maybe you have the same curiosity. Perhaps you've known someone for years and asked yourself, "That person is so gifted, talented, and charismatic—why haven't they accomplished more with their life?" Or maybe in the work environment, you've wondered, "So-and-so was on a fast track. Why were they passed up for promotions?"

The answer is simple. They stopped *learning* and stopped *growing*.

At some point in their life or career, they got lazy or complacent and stopped updating their skills. A pretty smart guy named Albert Einstein said, "Learning is not a product of schooling, but the lifetime attempt to acquire it."

Notice he said *lifetime*. Einstein also said, "Once you stop learning, you start dying." Personally, I'm not in favor of dying. (I'm shooting for 103 candles on my cake.)

Can't afford the time or tuition? Think again. Over 1,200 universities—including Harvard and Yale—now offer free online classes (see *edx.org*). Similar programs are offered from MIT, Stanford, Berkeley, Oxford, and more. One site alone offers 30,000 hours of free audio and video lectures (*openculture.com*).

Remember, the primary controllable determinant between success and failure in our second half is having or acquiring the right skills to go forward. Isaac Asimov pointed out, "Self-education is the only kind of education there is."

Are you as smart as a London cabdriver?

Every cabbie in central London must memorize 25,000 streets and thousands of landmarks before getting a license. Building this mental atlas takes three to four years of intense study.

But there's a payoff—a *bigger brain*. According to a report in *Current Biology*, learning London's maze of streets causes structural changes in the brain—improving memory and creating a greater volume of nerve cells in the brain's hippocampus. In a study at University College London, Eleanor Maguire and team followed a group of trainee taxi drivers. Using MRI shots of their brain structures, Maguire discovered that learning new skills actually built brain power and *size*.

That's great news for second-halfers. The human brain remains "plastic" even in adult life, allowing it to adapt as we learn new tasks.

In laymen's terms, our brain is either shrinking or growing. Lifelong learning increases gray matter. So keep learning. Keep sharpening the axe. Neural stimulation multiplies the number of synapses; stagnation reduces them.

I'm from the Motor City. And the man who put the world on wheels personally ran his company until he was 82 years old. Henry Ford never stopped learning. And he hung around others who kept learning and growing—like Thomas Edison and Harvey Firestone. Ford once said, "Anyone who stops learning is old, whether at 20 or 80. Anyone who keeps learning stays young."

# Don't Bury Your Dream.

As kids, most of us had a dream job in mind. Fireman, astronaut, ballerina, whatever. Sadly, as we grew up, many of us denied it and stuffed it down until it just went dormant within us.

But when we bury a dream, a part of *us* dies with it. All the things we could have accomplished, created, or performed will never happen if we bury our dream. Henry David Thoreau put it this way, "Most men lead lives of quiet desperation and go to the grave with their song still in them."

Here's the good news. We don't have to die with our music still inside of us. Regardless of your age, income, or education, grab a shovel and dig up the passion that stirs your soul and make *that* your life's work, your vocation—for as many years as you have left on this earth.

It's never too late to listen for your calling, chase it down, and build a legacy.

As a coach, I know that radical life change can be scary, especially if you're past middle age. Listening to the voice in us that says we can *be* more, *do* more, and *risk* more is scary. But it's not half as scary and depressing as getting to the end of your life, looking back, and regretting that you never followed your dream.

Working hard for something we don't care about is called "putting in time." Working hard for what we love is called "passion." There's a huge difference.

# Make a Lasting Impact.

Baby Boomers are brimming with talent. But what's the best way to use it?

If you're going to work during your second half, make sure you're pursuing something that gives you joy, satisfaction, and above all, purpose.

If doing endless, pointless activity describes your typical day, make a move. Use your second-half work stage as the chance to finish strong. If you didn't follow your passion during earlier seasons of life (for whatever reason), *now is the time* to shift gears—to finally do what you were created to do from the beginning.

As we saw in Section 4, my friend, Peter Thomas, is a super-achiever in business. But his passion is helping others through philanthropy. He encourages entrepreneurs to practice values-based leadership that gives back. "When you're blessed with the skills that are needed to become successful, along with that comes responsibility to help. I don't feel it's an obligation; it's an honor. One person can make a difference."

Thomas says purpose-driven generosity goes beyond finances. "I've coined a saying, 'When you have time, you give time. When you have money, you give money. When you have time and money, you give both.' I've always spent time giving back. It gives you an incredibly good feeling of being needed and wanted."

Thomas's idea of calling fits with theologian Frederick Beuchner's definition: "Vocation is that place where our deepest passion meets the world's greatest need." That can sound like a tall order. It can feel intimidating to consider our daily work in light of such a lofty goal. But the world—which includes our neighborhood community—has many needs, big and small, and there are many ways to meet them, big and small.

You don't have to change the entire world, just improve one small corner of it.

American novelist Wendell Barry said, "The old and honorable idea of 'vocation' is simply that we are each called by God, or by our gifts, or by our preference, to a kind of work for which we are particularly fitted."

Incidentally, the etymology of the word "vocation" is fascinating. It's rooted in the Latin word meaning "voice" or "to call." A vocation is not a career we pursue; it's a *calling we hear*. Think of it as a voice summoning you to your unique purpose.

———

As we've seen, the world would be far poorer if the aging titans of art, music, and science had hung up their tools and headed for the shuffleboard court. People like Renoir, Einstein, and Strauss never stopped improving. And neither should you. That's why my wife and I are voracious readers (she's working on her Ph.D.).

Granted, reading takes more effort than grabbing the remote, but the rewards are exponentially greater. I love surfing the web, watching TED Talks, and listening to podcasts. But *reading* is still the most effective way to satisfy my intellectual curiosity. Like Jim Rohn says, "Successful people have libraries. The rest have big screen TVs."

In her *Forbes* article, "Why Leaders Must Be Readers," Kelsey Meyer says, "Reading and learning from peers within and outside your industry enable you to grow in three ways." First, she notes, reading *reminds you.* "It keeps important concepts top of mind." Second, she says, reading *challenges you.* "Reading something you disagree with impacts your ability to think creatively and logically." Third, she says, reading *connects you,* by giving you opportunities to interact. It's a great tool to "share ideas and inspire action in each other."

One of the best ways to sharpen your axe is reading. You become smarter, more valuable to clients or employers, and more fun to be around. Leaders are readers, readers are leaders. It's that simple. And it's great for your brain health.

## Fitness Trumps Age.

After decades of government warnings, reams of medical research, and a barrage of public service ads, everybody with a brain knows the value of exercise and nutrition.

Yet many of us neglect our fitness.

Why do I bring this up? Because my plan for you is to have an extraordinary, intentional life—right up until you exit the planet. That means the proven linkage between lack of *fitness* and lack of *well-being* is especially critical once you're over age 55. If Boomers let their fitness slide, they can miss out on the joy of living at maximum velocity with energy and stamina.

As we saw, you and I have a good chance to live 35 to 40 percent longer than today's "average" life span. That's partly due to exponential progress in medicine and technology. *But even more important is taking care of ourselves.* It's great to have new high-tech fixes for things that go wrong in our body, but it's much better to avoid the crisis preemptively. Simple things like walking 30 minutes a day can make huge differences in the way we feel and look.

If we make it to age 100 or beyond—while enjoying a reasonably good quality of life as we go—it will mainly be because we did our part.

Perhaps you're thinking, "Great. If only I'd known that 20 or 30 years ago." If you play golf, you know a "mulligan" is a second chance to replay a bad shot. The concept applies to any situation where we're allowed to repeat an action that went wrong through blunder or poor performance. And it applies to our health. Regardless of what kind of life you've led, the effects of aging are reversible. You can have a do-over. Some are even saying that if you perform a good habit for thirty-six months, the benefits are almost as good as if you've done it your entire life.

## LEAVE A LEGACY

Setting five world records at a track and field event is amazing. Doing it at the age of 100 is even more amazing.

On a sweltering day in September 2015, Don Pellmann did exactly that—by setting new records for his age group in the high jump, long jump, shot put, discus, and hundred-meter dash.

Many centenarians can't even *walk* 100 meters, but Pellmann sprinted the distance in twenty-seven seconds, breaking the previous world record by three seconds.

Believe it or not, this wasn't the most records Pellmann has set in a single meet. In 2005, at age 90, he broke seven age-group records at a meet in Colorado.

Pellmann's been competing in senior track meets since he was 70. He's entered 890 events and has won gold medals in all but five of them. That's perseverance. So is this—he often competes against men 30 years younger. And that age gap seems to inspire him. "I like it when somebody says, 'I've been competing with you for 20 years and I'm getting sick of looking at your back.'"

Today at 103, Pellmann is destroying the myth about old age being a liability and a disqualification from active living. The feisty senior competes in a red T-shirt emblazoned with the words: "Donald Pellmann—Founded in 1915."

In my case, that was welcome news. I haven't always managed my fitness levels or nutrition the way I do now. But new science findings incentivize us to jump in regardless of age or past shortcomings. Apparently, within just *three months* of changing a behavior, there is a measurable increase in our potential life expectancy.

## Aging Is Inevitable, but the *Rate* Is Not.

Today, I watch what I eat, sleep eight hours, and stay physically active with a variety of outdoor and indoor activities that keep me in shape. There are three principles behind my workouts:

1. My exercises are so simple I can do them at home or in a hotel—I don't need a gym, so I never have an excuse to skip.

2. My focus is on building "core strength." With a strong core, I don't have back problems and hernias. At age 60, I can

snowmobile 400 miles in a day (2,000 miles in a week), and my back doesn't bother me.

3. I am leveraging the cumulative effect of this rhythm—10 years, 20 years, 30 years—knowing this simple model will pay exponential dividends as I grow into my later years.

Writer and academic, Germaine Greer, once said, "Nobody ages like anybody else." Aren't you glad? That quote should inspire you to do your part in being the exception to the cultural clichés of mandatory physical decline.

In grade school, I was told to "act my age." Not anymore. I refuse to be pigeonholed by ageism. So should you. The 79-year-old Greer also said, "You're only young once, but you can be immature forever." To that I say, *amen and pass the ski poles.* If somebody thinks I'm a little off the rails for wanting to ski a black diamond slope at age 90, then so be it.

One aim of my Legacy Map—my written goals—is to be fun, fit, and contributing to society until I'm at least 103.

I want to have the guts to say *age is only a number* and then prove it by living a life of passion and purpose.

Obviously, genetics play a part, and everyone's physiology is different. But even allowing for DNA anomalies, your body is basically a biological machine. And a thrifty one at that. We mentioned the maxim, *use it or lose it.* Turns out, it's medically accurate. Helpful things like muscle mass, brain cells, bone density, and libido all take a hike if you ignore them for long.

Your body is designed to conserve energy and resources at all costs, and it deletes whatever isn't being used.

So stay active. Stay in the game. Don't surrender.

## Movement Is Medicine.

True confession: Some mornings I don't feel like exercising. (Okay, make that *many* mornings.) But then I ask myself, "When I'm a nonagenarian, do I want to be sitting in a wheelchair or sitting in a ski lift with my grandkids? Do I want to be riding a rocking chair or riding my Yamaha dirt bike?"

I'm an aggressive snow skier, snowmobiler, and off-road explorer. And I don't ever want to give up that freedom of mobility because I sloughed off.

Life is all about choices, big and little. I can't control the future or change my genetic ancestry. But I *can* decide whether I skip a workout or not. Each time I choose fitness over inactivity, it reinforces my good habits. Same for you. We can work out or sell out—*It's too rainy, it's too hot, it's too cold. The football game is on, I'd rather go shopping. I'm tired, I'm bored, I'm hungry*, whatever.

Step by step, little by little, we give up, and the debilitating symptoms of a sedentary lifestyle creep in. Let me just say that you do not need an expensive trainer or a gym membership to stay fit. Someone has wisely said, *movement is medicine.* And it doesn't take a prescription.

Ever drive with a hot decaf sitting on your lap and hit the brakes? Coffee in motion stays in motion. Same for people. To be precise,

Newton's First Law says, "Objects in motion tend to stay in motion; objects at rest tend to stay at rest." So keep walking, gardening, dancing, swimming, biking, golfing, or kickboxing. It doesn't cost a fortune to stay healthy, just a change of attitude.

"Your body reads idleness as a sign that you are starving to death as slowly as possible, no matter how much you eat. Exercise." That advice is from Chris Crowley, co-author of *Younger Next Year: A Guide to Living Like 50 Until You're 80 and Beyond.*

His partner, Dr. Henry Lodge, sums up their rules for slowing the aging process:

1. Exercise six days a week for the rest of your life.

2. Do serious aerobic exercise four days a week for the rest of your life.

3. Do serious strength training two days a week for the rest of your life.

4. Spend less than you make.

5. Quit eating crap.

6. Care.

7. Connect and commit.

Active senior, Laura Carstensen, is director of the Stanford Center on Longevity. The 64-year-old psychology professor says, "Exercise and persistently trying to solve big problems is what keeps people sharp and makes life satisfying."

Am I a fitness expert? No.

Do I practice what I preach? Yes.

I want you and me to approach older age with optimism, resilience, and an awareness that thousands of enlightened (or stubborn) peers are proving that paradigms about aging were made to be broken. Reaching 103 (or 90 or 110 or whatever your personal goal is) won't be fun if you're not fit to enjoy life on your own terms. That's why I've spent so much time on the subject.

We won't all run fast or break records like Don Pellmann. But no matter how slow you go, you're still lapping anybody on the couch.

———

*"Physical fitness is not only one of the most important keys to a healthy body; it is the basis of dynamic and creative intellectual activity."*

—JOHN F. KENNEDY

# IT ALL COMES DOWN TO CHARACTER

## HOW TO NAVIGATE SAFELY AND CONFIDENTLY TO YOUR ENVISIONED FUTURE

*"People with good intentions make promises. People with good character keep them."*

—UNKNOWN

*"Character builds slowly, but it can be torn down with incredible swiftness."*

—FAITH BALDWIN

# Collision Course.

You may have heard the story of a confrontation that took place sometime after World War I, back before ships had high-tech radio communication.

It was dusk, and the captain remained on the bridge of a huge Navy battleship after a long day of training maneuvers. Because of the fog, the captain had stationed sailors at all the lookout posts. Suddenly, one of the men runs up to the captain, "Sir, we've spotted a light coming right at us. We're on a collision course!"

The captain orders a message be sent by Morse code. "Tell them, 'You are on a collision course. Advise you change your course by 20 degrees!'"

Immediately they get a response, "I suggest you change YOUR course by 20 degrees."

The captain is perturbed. He barks out an order, "Tell them 'I am a US Navy *captain*, and I advise you to change your course.'"

A response comes back, "I am a *second-class seaman* and I advise you to change your course."

By now, the captain is really angry. Furious, he says, "Tell them 'I am a 40,000-ton *battleship* and I advise you to change course NOW.'"

The response comes back, "I am a *lighthouse*, advise YOU change course now."

I don't care if we're a rowboat or an aircraft carrier armed to the teeth—if we compromise certain principles, we will run aground.

No matter how wealthy or powerful we are, we must follow our moral compass or risk collision. When I'm aligned with my list of principles, it's smooth sailing. But if I veer off—like being impatient or arrogant—I can crash right onto the rocks.

This story can be used to illustrate several other points. It may be our ship, but it's not our ocean. We've all got blind spots. Being stubborn can sink us. Being arrogant sets us up for humiliation. And most importantly, we can't control or change every situation—sometimes we need to divert. That's the beauty of having a Legacy Map infused with our best character traits to guide us.

———

Each of us is the captain of our own ship—that is, our life.

No sane captain would sail without his compass and charts. Same for negotiating the storms of everyday life. Stephen Covey said, "Principles are like a compass. A compass has a true north that is objective and external, that reflects natural laws or principles, as opposed to values which are subjective and internal."

These "true north" guiding principles are found in all six major world religions and are known as *self-evident, self-validating natural laws*. They show us the right direction for every facet of our existence. Just as a needle always swings to magnetic north, these laws are constant and apply at all times in all places.

Both in *7 Habits of Highly Effective People* and *Principle-Centered Leadership*, Covey emphasizes that all transformation must come from within. Achieving long-term effectiveness and impact hinges on his famous maxim, "Begin with the end in mind." Cultivating a legacy that outlives us requires a *lifetime perspective*—exactly the point of the Legacy Map strategy.

When individuals and societies operate in harmony with these laws, they prosper. When this "compass" is ignored, individuals fail, families suffer, companies falter, communities decay, and nations decline.

To be all we can be, we need to center our lives on true north principles. Religious or not, people instinctively trust an individual whose personality and behavior are grounded on this universal code of ethics. Ideally, subordinating ourselves to a *higher purpose* using *higher principles* is the foundation of effective leadership.

Covey sums it up in three resolutions:

1. Exercise self-discipline and self-denial.

2. Work on character and competence.

3. Dedicate your talents and resources to noble purposes and service to others.

We all need what I call a "character compass" reliably pointing the way. If we follow it, we won't get confused by conflicting voices and shifting values.

## Character Compass

Even the best map isn't much good without a compass. To navigate the Legacy Map you're creating, you'll need to consult your

Character Compass. Its dial is inscribed with four cardinal points of reference:

1. **Principles.** These ethical guidelines for human conduct steer your daily journey clear of the rocky shoals. *(Examples are integrity, humility, loyalty, courage, gratitude, dignity, fairness, honesty, etc.)*

2. **Core Values.** These shared values are co-created with your spouse and used by your family to navigate life's important decisions. *(Examples are trust, hard work, lifelong learning, spirituality, wisdom, intimacy, etc.)*

3. **Purpose.** The essential WHY behind every WHAT decision you make. It provides true north for life's journey and stays fundamentally constant your entire life.

4. **High Pay-off Activities.** This activity grid lets you check if you're on the right course overall, even when goals aren't being met on a short-term basis.

Now, let's unpack each of the four elements.

1. Stick to Your Principles.

Remember the story of the battleship headed for the rocks? No matter how big or successful we appear, we're all subject to certain immutable **Principles.**

My personal list of principles is how I navigate life. When I plan my day and make decisions based on those principles, I can be certain of safe passage. But if I disregard one or more of them, the journey becomes dangerous. I admit that when seas get rough, I'm tempted to cut corners or circumvent my principles. But if I do, my life, goals, and reputation are at risk of shipwreck.

Your principles can be both the qualities you *currently* possess and the qualities you are *aspiring* to. For example, I inherited "perseverance" from my father. So that was a given for me. No problem. I already possessed it. On the other hand, I'm lacking in "patience." My parents did not pass this down—in fact, I often watched my father explode with impatience and anger at daily challenges. That's my instinctive reaction, too. Whether it's triggered by traffic snarls or major adversity, I'm committed to overcoming this trait. So patience is on my list!

Remember, you have the rest of your life to work on self-improvement, so go ahead and list as many guiding principles as you identify with. Include those you currently possess, and the aspirational ones you're drawn to.

"Humility" is another principle on my list. I've always admired successful and confident leaders who model humility. On the flip side, I'm put off by ostentatious behavior. But despite my disdain for hubris, I too have been guilty of arrogance and condescension. My goal is to exhibit the appealing humility of someone like our second president, John Adams.

I still have a long way to go. But I've made progress over the past 20 years. And I'm (humbly) confident I'll continue for the next 20.

## John's Principles

1. Sobriety
2. Integrity
3. Courage
4. Humility
5. Service
6. Perseverance
7. Patience
8. Growth
9. Gratitude
10. Love

2. Finding Your Core.

**Core Values** are an *extension* of Principles, and in regard to the Legacy Map, they are specifically developed for your own particular family.

Early on, I utilized the concept of core values in my coaching and advising role (using content from Jim Collins). In my work with leadership teams, we uncover common core values that exist within the organization for the purpose of attracting and retaining individuals who share those values.

It's important to note that a job applicant cannot just "buy into" or acquire core values through osmosis. They are typically formed early, during our upbringing.

Core values are shaped by our parents and the environment we grow up in. Short of a major event (birth of a child, surviving cancer, etc.), they seldom change.

That's why Collins encouraged employers to find and hire people who are *already* predisposed to share a company's core values. Applicants who don't currently embrace them probably never will, so let them go elsewhere.

Based on that, I propose limiting the number of Legacy Map Core Values to just three or four. Each must meet two criteria: (1) If you're married, they are shared by you and your spouse; and (2) they were role-modeled by your parents.

For example, my wife, Molly, and I share the core value of "hard work." Our parents knew the value and joy of working, and we both inherited the deep satisfaction that comes from giving your best effort. In turn, we passed this same core value on to our children. They, too, will likely keep it for a lifetime.

## LEAVE A LEGACY

Carmen Herrera sold her first painting at the age of 89.

For most of her career, this Cuban woman's geometric paintings were ignored, even though male artists like Barnett Newman, Ellsworth Kelly, and Frank Stella became famous for similar artworks. Yet Carmen refused to give up. She had her core values and she was going to live by them, whether she was ever recognized or not. Every morning (after her *café con leche*), she sat down and painted at her work table, located at one end of the loft she lived in for 50 years. She attributes her lack of fame to being a woman in an age before they were recognized equally for their work. In 2016, at 101, Carmen Herrera's work was exhibited at London's Tate Gallery as well as the Museum of Modern Art and the Whitney Museum of American Art in New York. That's the kind of long-term dedication that ignores old age—and creates impact!

All of us are role-modeling our core values, whether we admit it or not. Back in 1993, NBA superstar, Charles Barkley, said, "I am not a role model." That controversial quip wound up in a Nike commercial. In a *Sports Illustrated* column, fellow hoopster Karl Malone pushed back, "Charles, you can deny being a role model all you want, but I don't think it's your decision to make. We don't choose to be role models, we are chosen. Our only choice is whether to be a good role model or a bad one."

Same for us. We can't opt out. Even if we're not fully *aware* of our core values, they're a huge part of who we are—and our families (and employees) are exposed to them every day.

The core values that you and your spouse have in common are likely the reason you were originally attracted to each other and why you respect each other. The goal now is to *identify* those common values! Doing that lets you articulate and impart them to your children (and grandchildren). When adversity comes, you can remind your offspring how to navigate difficult stages by relying on the family's previously established core values.

## John's Core Values

1. Hard work
2. Love of learning
3. Perseverance

3. Purpose-Driven Future.

Countless books show how to find or clarify your **Purpose**, including Rick Warren's *Purpose Driven Life* (which I recommend—over

100 million sold). In the opening line of his bestseller, Warren gives away the deceptively simple secret to a fulfilling life, "It's not about you."

As it pertains to your Legacy Map, I submit that purpose *provides lifetime direction, underpins why you exist, and inspires you to fulfill your mission.*

When you're expressing and living out your purpose, your life has meaning, direction, and endless energy. Instead of being frustrated by work, you'll be inspired to learn more, reach higher, and contribute increasing value.

Warning: Life isn't a bed of roses just because you find your purpose. There will always be challenges. At the end of each day, you will still be tired. You will still need vacations and rejuvenation time, but you will not be discouraged, drained, or burned out. When you're purpose-driven, you're drawing on an abundant source of energy called passion and enthusiasm.

Serving a cause greater than yourself allows you to get out of your own head (and ego) to address the "higher calling" on your life— the calling you were created for, the purpose you're on earth to accomplish. And because your purpose is divinely inspired, your work will never be totally finished.

When you die, you'll be both *mourned* for being gone and *respected* for your drive, focus, and contribution while alive. (Sound appealing? It should!)

Throughout this book, we've looked at many ways to find your purpose. Now in closing, let me give you some good news—it's been there all along! If you think back, it's probably shown up many times in constructive and value-adding ways. Ask yourself, "What have I done that's given me energy and enthusiasm? What have I done that's provided satisfaction from within and affirmation from without?"

(I had someone ask me similar questions—and I encourage you to try it.)

Reflecting on my life, there were many clues along the way. When I was a teenager trying to figure out the world, my father challenged me. "Find something you love to do because you're going to spend the rest of your life doing it." He underscored that point by declaring he wasn't going to support me financially. At the time, I was doing manual labor and working construction. Although I enjoyed the freedom the money provided me, I was not inspired by the job. I was simply working for the weekend when I could spend my wages.

During this period of manual labor, I met one of many mentors who would change my life. This coworker said that if he had *my* opportunities and potential, he would stop working construction and return to school. He said he would use his mind and not his body for his vocation. I respected his opinion and returned to college to complete my degree.

I knew his advice was wise. And I was grateful. But I still had no idea what my purpose was or what I was going to spend my life doing.

Up until then, my motivation was simply to create a financially secure lifestyle and have fun. But that prospect no longer seemed quite as satisfying.

I remembered my father's admonition about loving what you do so much that you could do it for life. I ran a mental checklist of things I loved doing—*downhill skiing, snowmobiling, dirt biking, and fast cars.* In fact, I loved driving any vehicle. On my construction job, I sometimes drove big truckloads of equipment from Michigan to Louisiana. That was fun, but I wasn't drawn to it as a lifelong vocation.

Next, I thought about the skiing idea; perhaps I could be a ski bum or work at a resort. Maybe I could become an instructor or join the ski patrol. Again, lots of visceral appeal, but I never pursued it past the dream stage.

Finally, I began zeroing in on my passion. And by proxy, my purpose.

I realized from my choice in athletics that I tended to prefer *solo* sports over team sports. (The exception was hockey. I loved racing around the rink on skates but didn't enjoy getting checked into the boards.) Something in me liked *navigating my own journey* and *being a leader.*

That instinct rose to the surface during a series of snowmobiling trips I planned, organized, and led for groups of outdoor enthusiasts.

Once I hatched the idea, I began recruiting potential riders. Sometimes I would meet someone with a similar passion for fast vehicles; maybe they had a sports car or rode a motorcycle. Perhaps they even snowmobiled in the past but hadn't ridden for years. I discovered I could ignite or rekindle their passion. I could literally see interest and curiosity build as I described in exciting detail the trails we'd ride, machines we'd rent, and the sheer adventure of the weekend.

When I expressed a vivid vision of a future event, they wanted in! It was clear from my time at IBM that I was obviously good at selling people on intangible ideas. My success at recruiting riders was validation of that gift.

The next step after generating interest was getting a solid commitment. This involved collecting a deposit from prospective riders by Labor Day to secure the best rentals and lock in the dates. After that, I went into preparation mode, emailing precise clothing requirements and trip expectations. I provided details about what to expect and how to properly prepare mentally and physically. As early winter arrived, I sent periodic weather reports, trail conditions, and hotel information to keep the group engaged and excited.

Finally, the last logistics were confirmed and the trip was on.

During the excursions, I was always the leader. I rented the sleds, charted the course, and ran the group each day. I memorized the routes in advance, so I wouldn't need to break momentum to check maps. I studied detours to skirt impassable trails, if needed. I planned out the most scenic stops by streams or hills for maximum vistas. Finally, if we were headed for a fallen tree or any potentially damaging obstacle, I would arrive first and help my riders avoid the danger.

This attention to detail and level of responsibility were related to both my passion and my purpose. I didn't know it at the time, but what I was actually doing in this leisure activity was living out my purpose: *inspiring and challenging leaders to achieve their greatest personal potential!*

It was all in the context of a snowmobile experience, but it was an uncanny precursor of my current calling—I was visualizing for them an experience they had not yet personally been through. I was charting the course for them to follow. I was coaching them before and during the journey. I was ensuring they arrived safely at their destination (to the extent that it was within my control). I was leading from the front and not asking them to do anything I wasn't willing to do myself.

Each trip was both challenging and inspiring, an experience that pushed all of us out of our comfort zone. By the end of each run, we had inevitably broken through a new limitation or ceiling of complexity.

Those snowy trips paralleled the coaching work I do today with clients. They also set the stage for the Legacy Map process and the book you're reading.

The kind of unique purpose I found while planning those trips is somewhere in *your* life too, always calling (or whispering) to you. If you take the time to listen, it can bring you to a self-awareness of your destiny and direction for life.

The fact that *purpose* is often rolled up inside *passion* is by design!

Your calling—cloaked or in plain sight—can provide meaning and direction. It can bring joy and energy. But in many cases, it may not align with your current career.

When I worked in sales at IBM, I was flirting with aspects of my purpose. As CEO of Gorman's Business Interiors, I was even closer. With each step, I was getting nearer to manifesting my purpose within The CEO Advantage and my Legacy Map program.

Hopefully, my example will nudge you to consider your passions—to compare what you love most with what you're doing now on a daily basis.

## John's Purpose

**To inspire and challenge leaders to achieve their greatest personal potential.**

4. Making It Pay Off.

Your list of **High Pay-Off Activities** should be the personal and professional activities that make best use of your valuable and limited time. Defining them, listing them, and reviewing them often will act as a navigation aid in life.

Many of us have calendars, day planners, and sticky notes jammed with demands on our time. But as we saw earlier, when it comes to goal setting, *less is more.* That's why we suggest chopping your "to-do list" down to a manageable group of six priorities with specific goals to accomplish them, ranked in importance from one to six.

The most effective way to achieve your goals boils down to three steps: (1) *limit them*; (2) *rank them*; and (3) *work on them in that order as much as possible.*

Here's the challenge: on any given day, it can be difficult or impossible to accomplish even a narrowly focused list of six or fewer goals.

Unexpected issues, customer demands, and urgent pressures all compete for your limited time. When the smoke clears, you're left wondering if you accomplished anything worthwhile. Checking your actions against your high pay-off activities list lets you look back on the day or the week and gauge what actually happened.

In light of your high pay-off activities, you may find that what seemed off-mission and disorganized was actually useful, and that you made more progress than you thought. If you work on leveraging your time spent in high pay-off activities, you can be confident you're still tracking with your lifetime priorities—even if you technically fail to complete your top three to six action items for the week.

Want more good news? You will find your goals and specific action items frequently *encompass* your high pay-off activities, so there is overall alignment. The rationale for high pay-off activities comes from Stephen Covey's *7 Habits* book. For example, let's say you schedule the review of an unproductive employee (or unruly child) into a nice, neat, one-hour time slot. Of course, the time required to properly conduct a disciplinary meeting isn't predictable, so it might go over. Don't sweat it.

When personal or business issues don't fit your allocated slot (but *are* in alignment with your high pay-off activities), no problem. You are still on the right path.

# John's High Pay-off Activities

**Personal Activities:**

1. Further develop healthy daily habits to incorporate into my life (affirmations, self-talk, vision board w/BHAG always visible to inspire me daily)
2. Loving Molly, children, extended family, friends through activity, time, listening, value enhancement, knowledge sharing
3. Protecting my confidence by engaging in rejuvenation activities that hone my mind, thinking, push healthy boundaries (snowmobile, expert skiing, rafting, etc.)
4. Role model the Legacy Map as the tool that enhances life after 50 (make it really work for me and others close to me)
5. Define and articulate my self-worth so I know it from the inside out, not the outside in

**Professional Activities:**

1. Growing existing relationships (w/focus on high leverage relationships, like Warren) - will make list by category
2. Working on project 10X as best vehicle to scale my content, brand, wealth
3. Driving more value for my existing CEOA clients
4. Develop habit of writing & publishing BLOG - book
5. Sharpening my skills (focus on value creation, sales, coaching, listening)

# Character Takes Time.

Society's conversation about what constitutes "character" today is confusing. Role models range from sports figures to pop stars to fashion models. Some are decent and upright; others are shameless taboo-breakers. But whether noble or ignoble, one thing is certain— a person's character is often clearly distinct from personality, public image, reputation, or celebrity status.

In his book, *Character Counts*, Os Guinness says, "It is the essential stuff a person is made of, the inner reality and quality in which thoughts, speech, decisions, behavior, and relations are rooted." So a person's character expresses most deeply what constitutes them as a unique individual.

Which is why you can't read a person's character from a brief encounter. Or a press release. Or a third-party conversation. Guinness says, "A person's core character is best seen in what he or she reveals consistently rather than a single statement or random act."

Nietzsche calls these consistent habits, "a long obedience in the same direction."

That's our goal, too. A *lifelong journey* of consistently shaping our character by practicing the principles and core values that help us navigate our Legacy Map.

Peggy Noonan, a speechwriter for Ronald Reagan, said, "In a president, character is everything...He doesn't have to be clever; you can hire clever...But you can't buy courage and decency; you can't rent a strong moral sense."

## LEAVE A LEGACY

One leader with a strong moral sense was General George Marshall, America's foremost soldier and statesman during World War II and beyond. He was Army Chief of Staff under presidents FDR and Truman, and later served as Secretary of State and Secretary of Defense (no one else has held all three offices). From 1939 to 1945, Marshall built up and deployed the world's largest army—eight million soldiers. Winston Churchill called him the "organizer of victory." After the war, he won the Nobel Prize for formulating the Marshall Plan to rebuild Europe.

One story sums up his character. When Roosevelt asked if Marshall wanted to lead Operation Overlord—the D-Day invasion—he refused to promote himself. Forgoing personal ambition, the five-star general told FDR to do what was best for the country. Roosevelt gave the honor to Dwight D. Eisenhower. Marshall humbly turned down the greatest command in history, and never once complained about being passed over. Marshall's "character compass" demanded unwavering honesty and transparency in himself and others. "Go right straight down the road, to do what is best, and to do it frankly and without evasion."

The role of the Character Compass is to define us, inspire us, and guide our thoughts, speech, and actions. Use it in conjunction with your Lifetime, Annual, and Quarterly goals to help navigate your Legacy Map. Like an actual magnetic compass, it will help you see where you are and plan where you're headed.

Enjoy the journey *and* the destinations as you live your legacy day by day.

# Managing Your Time.

We're all allotted the exact same twenty-four hours in a day. Then why do some people accomplish so much more than others?

Because they manage their nonessential activity.

That makes sense, but staying on task isn't easy. According to an article in *All Business* by Susan Wilson Solovic, companies lose $650 billion annually in productivity because of workplace distractions. Solovic says, "Statistics show an average worker starts a project and spends about 11 seconds on it before being distracted. Then it takes another 25 minutes before he or she gets back on track."

Today, being distracted is not only normal, it's *expected*.

How is it possible to cope with the avalanche of competing tasks that demand our immediate attention?

Stephen Covey's deceptively simple answer is found in *7 Habits of Highly Effective People*: "Most of us spend too much time on what's urgent and not enough on what's important." He wrote that 30 years ago, and it's still true! He expanded the idea in a later book co-written with Roger Merrill called, *First Things First*.

To help leaders maximize their efficiency, Covey popularized the concept of the Time Management Matrix. His four quadrants help prioritize which activities are absolutely necessary and which are merely distractions. Let's focus on one and two:

- **Quadrant 1** is for *important, urgent* items. Expected or unexpected, these need to be dealt with immediately. (Pressing business, last-minute preparations, genuine crises, hard deadlines, family emergencies, etc.)

- **Quadrant 2** is for *important but nonurgent* items. These don't require your immediate attention but need to be planned for (education, exercise, relationships, strategic direction, recreation, Legacy Map, etc.).

Obviously, Quadrant 1 is critical to success. But if we focus only on the operative aspect, we neglect our strategic perspective on things that matter most. Quadrant 2 is the greenhouse for cultivating essential Legacy Map skills like character development, values clarification, health awareness, relationship building, and lifelong learning.

Covey went so far as to say *all* progress is made in Quadrant 2. I agree. What we do in Quadrant 1 is basically just keeping up with work, problems, and deadlines. You don't push yourself forward unless you move to Quadrant 2.

For instance, writing this book is a Quadrant 2 activity. That's why I schedule it in the morning. If I don't set aside *specific time* to write (a form of visioning), I'll use the same excuse as some of my clients—"Too busy with Quadrant 1 to leave it."

Visioning is a Quadrant 2 activity that requires us to intentionally book time for it. It also requires *disciplined focus* and *creative thinking*. That means it will come easier for some and harder for others. Even though a person is successful and intelligent, a basic visioning exercise can be daunting—and they often avoid doing it.

That's where using a coach will bring a huge return on investment. Most coaches are wired like me—we love visioning! We actually find joy and purpose in helping others create, achieve, and remain consistently committed to a vision and related goals. Having a coach on your side reinforces your willpower and encourages you to "walk the talk." If you find yourself struggling, remember this—we all need a coach and/or mentor to motivate us to remain committed.

# Why Character Counts.

To make the most of your second half, you'll need a foundation of solid character principles to guide your choices.

Stephen Covey's *7 Habits* has sold 25 million copies. Researching it, Covey found that for our first 150 years, America's focus was on what he called "character ethics"—virtues like integrity, humility, loyalty, courage, justice, patience, industry, simplicity, modesty, and the Golden Rule.

This changed after World War I. The strategy for achieving success shifted to "personality ethics"—with an emphasis on public relations, positive thinking, and verbal skills. Leaders were taught to be persuasive, charming, and have a commanding personal appearance (remember the power tie?).

The landmark book suggested that character ethics deal with internal or core values, while personality ethics deal with external or superficial values. Penned twenty-six years after Covey's magnum opus, a book called *The Road to Character* by David Brooks also talks about the inner and outer set of ethics.

Brooks calls these two sets of ethics the "résumé virtues" and the "eulogy virtues." He says, "The résumé virtues are the skills you bring to the marketplace. The eulogy virtues are the ones talked about at your funeral—whether you were kind, brave, honest or faithful. Were you capable of deep love?"

Imagining your own funeral is a good exercise. *What will people remember me for after I'm gone?* Brooks says, "Our culture and educational systems spend more time teaching the skills and strategies you need for career success than the qualities you need to radiate that inner light. Many of us are clearer on how to build an external career than on how to build inner character."

Today, you can usually get by with a good résumé (what Covey calls personality ethics). But Brooks says you'll pay a price. "If you live for external achievement, years pass and the deepest parts of you go unexplored and unstructured. You lack a moral vocabulary. It is easy to slip into a self-satisfied moral mediocrity."

The consequence is to miss your calling. To endure what Thoreau called a life of "quiet desperation."

Brooks agrees, "You figure as long as you are not obviously hurting anybody and people seem to like you, you must be okay. But you live with an unconscious boredom, separated from the deepest meaning of life and the highest moral joys."

Each of us will face what Covey dubbed "a character moment." Under extreme pressure, it's our underlying values that will pull us through and sustain us. If we don't have a solid character ethic, virtue goes out the window, and we resort to tricks, techniques, and pragmatism (think about the charming but conniving characters in TV's *Mad Men*).

Ultimately, it's our character that communicates most eloquently. As Emerson quipped, "What you *are* shouts so loudly in my ears I cannot hear what you *say*."

I won't mention names, but we can all think of sports figures, politicians, and celebrities who have amazing, charismatic personalities and achieved enormous fame. Yet in a "character moment," they crashed and burned in public scandal.

What they all had in common was moral failure based on lack of character. They lacked vision of *who* they wanted to be in the future or *what* they wanted to leave as their legacy.

You're reading this book because you prefer a life of depth and meaning that honors others over a life of posturing and self-promotion.

If not, I challenge you to rebalance the scales—to emphasize inner qualities like kindness, bravery, honesty, and faithfulness during your second half.

## In Conclusion: No Regrets.

Congratulations on your self-investment.

Your time and energy will be repaid a thousand times over. You're part of a growing group of independent thinkers who refuse to settle for a linear existence. I'm excited to think about the purposeful goals you're setting and the attainable steps you're taking to change your world.

In his book, *Essentialism*, Greg McKeown urges us to pare down the nonessential activities that chip away at what he calls our "pathetically tiny amount of time" on this earth. He challenges us to be "unreasonably selective about how to use this precious time."

Using a Legacy Map is basically saying yes to what matters most, and no to everything else. McKeown agrees, "If you don't prioritize your life, someone else will." His plan is simple, "Whatever decision or challenge or crossroad you face in your life, simply ask yourself, 'What is essential?' Eliminate everything else."

My goal—and hopefully, yours—is a life finished without regret.

The key is making good choices. McKeown says, "If you have correctly identified what really matters, if you invest your time and energy in it, then it is difficult to regret the choices you make. You become proud of the life you have chosen."

You wouldn't get on a bus with a destination sign that read: "SOMEWHERE DOWN THE ROAD." Nor should you approach life with the same reckless attitude.

That's why you're engaged in crafting your life vision and mapping a path to your personal and professional dreams. You've learned that character growth, life satisfaction, and healthy aging don't happen automatically. Instead of retreating from change or sticking your head in the sand, you're intentionally leading from the front.

You know that creating a razor-sharp vision of the future you want is the only effective strategy for achieving it. You know that a second-half life of meaning and fulfillment does not happen by chance, but by design. And most importantly, you know that *replacing retirement with intentional living* is the key to it all.

Together, let's make choices that propel us toward our best future.

———

*"Character is the real foundation of all worthwhile success."*

—JOHN HAYS HAMMOND

# ABOUT THE AUTHOR

## John D. Anderson

For two decades, John Anderson has pursued one unchanging goal: *to inspire and challenge leaders to achieve their greatest personal potential.*

To that end, Anderson cofounded The CEO Advantage, a coaching and consulting firm designed to help fast growth organizations translate vision into execution and results.

Anderson gained early experience at IBM and later as CEO of Gorman's Business Interiors. In 1996, he founded the Detroit Chapter of the Entrepreneurs' Organization. Soon after, Verne Harnish chose Anderson to be his first coach in what is now Gazelles International. This led to launching The CEO Advantage in 1999 and ultimately to the Legacy Map—a visioning tool he created in 2008 to help leaders reach high levels of professional success and personal impact.

Believing in the power of aligned purpose and behavior, Anderson first used the Legacy Map to facilitate peak performance in the *corporate* setting. He was later inspired to transfer that same approach to *individuals.* Anderson now shares his life-focusing tools through one-on-one coaching, targeted seminars, and online access to visioning resources.

In 2012, John Anderson set out to change the national conversation on second-half living. His first book, *Replace Retirement: Living*

*Your Legacy in the Exponential Age,* is a manifesto on why America's economic health depends on people over 50 disrupting the current model and transforming the workplace by leveraging exponential technologies.

In addition to coaching and writing, he delivers high-content presentations and videos created to trigger possibility thinking and transformation. Readers can contact him, access his blog, and download their own Legacy Map at *ReplaceRetirement.com.*

An avid entrepreneur, Anderson holds equity positions in multiple businesses and interacts regularly with industry thought leaders. He keeps fit by skiing, snowmobiling, and doing other outdoor activities. He and his wife, Molly, divide their time between homes in Grand Rapids and Northern Michigan.

# ABOUT THE EDITOR

## Karl Nilsson

Detroit native, Karl Nilsson, enjoys collaborating with authors who challenge their readers to pursue a life of true significance and lasting impact.

Ten years ago, Nilsson paired up with Jeff Petherick to "publish the positive" by launching Elk Lake Publishing. The duo sought to inspire others by writing motivational books *Wavelength, Grace Like Rain,* and *Bigger than the Sky.*

Nilsson later coauthored *Life in the Balance: 7 Strategies for Making Life Work* with Michael Komara, and *Man Quest* with Mike McCormick. Beyond his nonfiction catalog, he has written numerous novels, stage plays, and film treatments.

Projects include travelling to Nepal to produce a video on human trafficking for Forgotten Children Worldwide. In addition to writing and editing, Nilsson consults business leaders and nonprofits on branding their story with persuasive language.

Prior to being communication director at the multisite Kensington Church, he was a syndicated cartoonist, newspaper columnist, and magazine editor.

Anderson's passion for goal setting drew Nilsson in. "John wants Americans of all ages to take charge of their futures and never stop adding value. As a Boomer myself, his idea of replacing retirement with an active, vibrant second half was a wake-up call."

Nilsson attended Wayne State's Monteith College. A former race driver, he loves all things Motown—from the area's cultural heritage to the motorsports. He also enjoys bicycling, boating, and exploring Michigan's backroads in his vintage Mustang.

He and his wife, Marie, have two adult children, Britt and Karl.

# LEGACY MAP

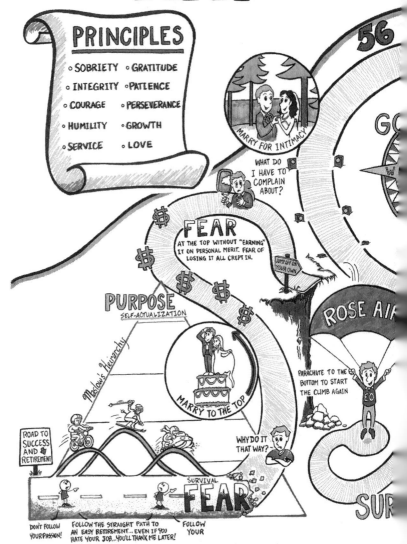

# JOHN'S VISION NARRATIVE

**July 1, 2026**

*What a glorious morning I have arrived at by living faithfully to God's will, being true to my purpose, and principles. I am grateful each morning for my sober life which is foundational to my peace and joy. Molly and I are grateful in both where we have been and where we are going and certainly today is yet another important milestone on that journey. The tremendous success and appeal of my first book inspired baby boomers and Americans over the age of 50 to embrace our MTP of "replacing retirement with intentional living." This purpose became a call to action and rallying point for re engaging the concept of personal freedom and self-worth in Americans over 50. The combination of the book and website created a vehicle for entrepreneurial thinking for boomers to make the second half of their life more impactful and fulfilling than the first half. The ripple impact on society was enormous in terms of the contribution of the boomer generation and their role modeling for younger generations.*

*The success of my first book was a result of several parallel synergistic events. First, readers identified with the multiple examples of others who have made the second half of their life more significant, meaningful, and enjoyable then the first half. Coupled with the evidence of exponential technologies enhancing the quality and duration of life and the step by step guide outlined in Replace Retirement, Living*

*Your Legacy in the Exponential Age, created a pathway for success and significance. Publishing the book also created market demand for my speaking with YPO, EO, AMAC, AARP, Gazelles and other organizations where I could personally share the vision and journey of enhancing the second half of life by replacing retirement with intentional living. My value and enjoyment as a speaker increased with each engagement attracting opportunities for over $25K per event plus expenses. These speaking engagements enabled Molly and I to travel to destinations that aligned with our own desired travel experiences. A significant contributor to the book's success and appeal was McKeel Hagerty writing the introduction and then going on to co-write a follow up book reinforcing the contribution and value of the second half of life. I received "super credibility" with the endorsement of Verne Harnish, Peter Diamandis, Ari Weinzweig, Dan Sullivan, David Brooks, David McCullough, Jack Stack, Pat Lencioni, Josh Linkner, Paul Akers, and others accelerating my book to New York Times bestselling status. The impact was beyond my wildest imagination.*

*The success of our MTP was a synergistic alliance of the skills and the valued input and navigation of the Replace Retirement Team. Each of the team signed on and initially volunteered their time in return for an equity and/or a revenue stake in the outcome. The ExO design of our business model allowed specific players each contributing their unique ability to invest time and resources because of their emotional attachment to the vision. By leveraging our efforts, energy, knowledge, and relationships we accelerated our mutual results and success. I acted as CVO continuing to write while leveraging my social capital attracting investors, clients, and strategic partners. Steve Wojno signed on as our COO/CFO providing two crucial elements to our ongoing growth. First Steve provided financial acumen and leadership to insure our goals aligned with our financial plan. Additionally, he provided the integration skills necessary to orchestrate the many moving parts keeping us accountable to timelines and deliverables. He helped in co-facilitating our strategy sessions as well as sharing his personal experience with a technology startup that failed to insure we didn't share a similar fate. Karl contributed by taking my initial content and polishing it with stories and emotional connection for our readers. We developed video's providing content to reinforce the tools online in addition to generating millions of web-based followers through an engaging video series. Tom Crimp and the Auxiliary team provided the marketing expertise and polish to make our website powerful, interactive, professional, and current. Working closely with Auxiliary we aligned all our brand and marketing across presentations, the book, the web, and videos to seamlessly deliver value to our following of over 1 million members and growing.*

*The Replace Retirement web-based tools coupled with Legacy Forum coaching enabled our online members to apply exponential thinking and attitudes to clarify their role and contribution to society. Those individuals' unique contributions showed up as improved health, wealth, and wellbeing. Our community members carry the banner of interdependence in choosing to define and articulate a clear path and plan of how they make a lasting and meaningful impact during the second half of life. By clearly articulating a path to follow with purpose, meaning, and contribution it changed the paradigm of what retirement meant from a time of contributing less to a time of contributing more. This improved lifestyle of physical, mental, and spiritual exercise resulted in reversing the trend of increasing healthcare costs. The collective financial contribution in the form of non-contractual 1099 employment and/or volunteering of time and wisdom substantially reduced the burden on society removing traditional employment contracts and benefits. This contribution freed* up greater opportunities for millennials to engage in more traditional employer/employee agreements.

Users of our online tools are served in multiple ways. Those opting for the free tools easily create a Vision Board on the Legacy Map platform to visually communicate what matters most in their personal and professional lives. Members who choose to go deeper develop a detailed narrative vision (story) for their life. As members create clarity around why living their legacy matters the next step is to create specific goals reinforced with daily habits that create alignment with their personal vision. Our automated tools allow members to create specific actionable goals to facilitate daily alignment or habits reinforced by mobile reminders to activate and measure progress towards their envisioned future.

Approximately 20% of our members enroll in personal coaching via our web-based Legacy Forum interactive coaching model. The Legacy Forum peer groups facilitated by our coaching community greatly enhance the goals, results, and engagement of our members in meaningful ways we did not fully grasp at the launch stage. The formation of the Legacy Forum communities created value and results far exceeding our expectations. Individual members were deeply impacted by the relationships they develop, and lives are forever changed through small but significant positive relationships. The coaches grew both out of our user base as well as from Gazelles, Financial Investment Advisors, and other coach-based platforms. This enhanced the quality of life for our coach community by role modeling a way of living that engages our members. Doorways of opportunities opened through the forum community further enhancing the value of the monthly engagement. More recently with the advent of virtual and augmented reality we have been leaders in utilizing interactive online communities to *reinforce engaging and living a personal vision. Our use of leading edge technologies has attracted investors and strategic partners who realize the leverage of immersing people in an augmented reality of their personal envisioned future.*

*The impact of this worthy goal created abundance in several unique ways. I was able to role model a lifestyle and thereby enhance my own life by continually increasing my health, contribution, relationships, and financial freedom. The value of Replace Retirement, LLC has exceeded $100M resulting in financial abundance for Molly, I, and our investors. As a faithful steward Molly and I determine suitable institutions that align with our vision to contribute 100% of our net worth in excess of our lifetime goal of $20M where we can make a direct impact on improving the lives of others and enrich a society that contributes in all seasons of life. Additionally, I remain committed to lifelong writing and content creation to achieve mastery and thought leadership as the go-to source for exponential growth after age 50. My life is dedicated to helping others to live lives of creativity and contribution maximizing their own unique ability. God has blessed me and my family in so many abundant ways and I am grateful to be his servant in this worthy cause and journey.*

# REFERENCES

## FOREWORD

Darren Hardy. *The Compound Effect*. Vanguard Press, 2011.

Richard Rohr. *Falling Upward: A Spirituality for the Two Halves of Life*. Jossey-Bass, 2011.

## INTRODUCTION

Verne Harnish. *Scaling Up: How a Few Companies Make It and Why the Rest Don't*. Gazelles Inc., 2014.

Entrepreneurs' Organization™ (EO) is a global nonprofit helping 11,000 leading entrepreneurs learn and grow through peer-to-peer learning and connections to experts. It was founded in 1987 by Verne Harnish. Learn more at *eonetwork.net*.

Gazelles International™ is a worldwide association of professional business coaches assisting companies with growth tools based on *Scaling Up* by founder Verne Harnish. Learn more at *gicoaches.com*. Get info on books, resources, and upcoming growth summits at *gazelles.com*.

## SECTION 1–The Exponential Revolution

Patrick Lencioni. *The Five Temptations of a CEO: A Leadership Fable.* Jossey-Bass, 1998.

The Table Group™ was founded in 1997 by Patrick Lencioni to spread organizational health to the world. They offer resources, videos, and consulting services for leaders. Lencioni was named "one of America's top five speakers" by the *Wall Street Journal.* Meet the Table Group™ at *tablegroup.com*

Marshall Goldsmith. *What Got You Here, Won't Get You There.* Hyperion Press, 2007.

Jim Rohn. *Leading an Inspired Life.* Nightingale-Conant, 1996.

James Vaupel, PhD. "Ageing Populations: The Challenge Ahead," *The Lancet.* October 3, 2009, Volume 374, Number 9696 (pgs. 1196-1208).

"Life Expectancy in the USA Hits New High," *USA Today.* October 9, 2014, by Larry Copeland.

David McCullough. *The Wright Brothers.* Simon & Schuster, 2015.

"When Man & Machine Merge," *Rolling Stone.* February 19, 2009, by David Kushner.

"Airlines to Welcome 3.6 Billion Passengers in 2016," International Air Transport Associates Press Release, December 6, 2012. (IATA data at *iata.org/pressroom.*)

Ric Edelman, *Truth about Money* radio show. "Ric Talks with XPRIZE Chairman and CEO Peter Diamandis" (November 16, 2015), and "How Exponential Technologies Could Affect Your Retirement Plans" (December 1, 2015). Listen at *edelman-financial.com/radio*.

Ray Kurzweil. "The Law of Accelerating Returns," *Kurzweil Accelerating Intelligence*, March 7, 2001 (*kurzweilai.net/the-law-of-accelerating-returns*).

"Five Things to Know About 5G," Mashable.com, February 8, 2018, by Karissa Bell.

Paul Taylor, Pew Research Center. *The Next America: Boomers, Millennials, and the Looming Generational Showdown*. Public Affairs Publishing, 2014.

"Millennials Overtake Baby Boomers as America's Largest Generation," *Pew Research Center*. April 25, 2016, by Richard Fry (*pewresearch.org/fact-tank*).

Peter Diamandis, multiple references drawn from Singularity University articles and posts. For similar updates, go to *su.org*.

"1.2 Billion Vehicles on World's Roads Now, 2 Billion by 2035," *Green Car Reports*. July 29, 2014, by John Voelcker (also quoting Ward's Automotive).

"Self-Driving Cars Could Cut Down Accidents, Study Says," *The Wall Street Journal*. March 5, 2005, by Mike Ramsey.

"Autonomous Car Forecasts," *Driverless Future*. April 10, 2016. Archives of recent predictions and news alerts regarding self-driving autos at *driverless-future.com*.

"A Bold Look at Moore's Law," *Forbes*. March 23, 2005, by Rich Karlgaard.

Rich Karlgaard and Michael Malone. *Team Genius: The New Science of High-Performing Organizations*. Harper Collins, 2015.

Peter Diamandis and Steven Kotler. *Bold: How to Go Big, Create Wealth, and Impact the World*. Simon & Schuster, 2015.

Peter Diamandis and Steven Kotler. *Abundance: The Future Is Better Than You Think*. Free Press, a division of Simon & Schuster, 2012.

Salim Ismail with Michael S. Malone and Yuri Van Geest. *Exponential Organizations: Why New Organizations Are Ten Times Better, Faster, and Cheaper Than Yours*. Diversion Books, 2014.

"Will 100 Be the New 60? Biotech Startup Human Longevity Thinks So," *CBS News*, March 5, 2014 (*cbsnews.com*).

"A Genetic Entrepreneur Sets His Sights on Aging and Death," *New York Times*, March 4, 2014, by Andrew Pollack.

"The Biggest Ship in the World (Though It Isn't Exactly a Ship)," *New York Times Magazine*. October 21, 2014, by Robert Sullivan.

"The Battery Pioneer Who, at Age 96, Keeps Going and Going," *Wall Street Journal*. August 9, 2018, by Sarah McFarlane.

'A Decade of Mass Extinction Event in S&P 500," *CNBC Exponential Finance*. June 5, 2012, by Lori Ioannou (interview with Peter Diamandis).

"The Re-Education of Jim Collins," *Inc.* magazine. October 1, 2013, by Bo Burlingham, Editor.

## SECTION 2—Live Long and Prosper

"So Paul McCartney is sixty-four. Now What?" *New York Times*, June 17, 2006, by Sam Roberts.

"Beatles Business: Still Making Money, 50 Years On," *CNBC*. February 7, 2014, by Mark Koba.

"Why 'Mad Men' Paid $250,000 to Use One Beatles Song," *Business Insider*. April 10, 2014, by Frank Pallotta.

All estimated celebrity income figures from *Celebrity Net Worth*. Accessed at *celebritynetworth.com*.

"The Evolution of Adulthood: A New Stage," *Center for Productive Longevity*, March 2000, by Dr. Elliott Jaques and William K. Zinke (*ctrpl.org*).

"This List Proves You're Never Too Old To Do Something Amazing," *Business Insider*. March 14, 2014, by Dan Waldschmidt. Edited excerpts from *Edgy Conversations* (see next reference, below).

Dan Walderschmidt. *Edgy Conversation: How Ordinary People Can Achieve Outrageous Success*. New Century Publishing, 2014.

Dr. Aubrey De Guy and Michael Rae, *Ending Aging: The Rejuvenation Breakthroughs That Could Reverse Human Aging in Our Lifetime*. St. Martin's Press, 2007.

"Dawn of a New Age: First Person to Reach 150 is Already Alive," *UK Daily Mail*. July 6, 2011. Quoting Dr. Aubrey De Grey.

"Who Wants to Live Forever? Scientist Sees Aging Cured," *Reuters Science News*, July 4, 2011, by Kate Kelland.

"Will 100 Be the New 60? Biotech Startup Human Longevity Thinks So," *CBS News*, March 5, 2014 (*cbsnews.com*).

References from Human Longevity cofounders Craig Venter, Ph.D. and Peter Diamandis, MD, are from their website, *humanlongevity.com*.

"Author and Physician Shigeaki Hinohara," *The Japan Times*. January 29, 2009, by Judit Kawaguchi.

"Millennials Overtake Baby Boomers as America's Largest Generation," *Pew Research Center*. April 25, 2016, by Richard Fry (*pewresearch.org/fact-tank*).

Diana Farrel et. al. "Talkin' 'bout my generation: The economic impact of aging baby boomers." *McKinsey Global Institute*, 2008.

"The End of Old," *Merrill Lynch Advisor*. 2014 Issue, by Anita Slomski.

Dan Sullivan, *The Laws of Lifetime Growth: Always Make Your Future Bigger Than Your Past*. The Strategic Coach, 2016.

Dan Sullivan, Catherine Numura, Julia Waller, and Shannon Waller. *Unique Ability: Creating the Life You Want.* The Strategic Coach, 2003.

"Unique Ability'" resources and downloads at *uniqueability.com.* Dan Sullivan's Strategic Coach team explains how finding the heart of who you are is the secret to your success, quality of life, and contribution to the world.

"Healthy Retired Nurse Ends Her Life Because Old Age Is No Fun," *The Telegraph.* August 2, 2015, by Laura Donnelly.

Some references for Woody Allen and Clint Eastwood drawn from online biographies at International Movie Database. Great info at *imbd.com.*

"An Interview with Woody Allen," *Wall Street Journal.* July 8, 2015, by Don Steinberg.

"Clint Eastwood Reflects On Age, America, and Acting," *Park Record.* June 16, 2014, by AP Film Writer Jake Coyle.

Isaac Stern and Chaim Potok, *My First 79 Years.* Knopf, 1999.

"The Truth About Entrepreneurs: Twice As Many Are Over 50 As Are Under 25," *PBS Newshour.* April 26, 2013 blogged by Vivek Wadhwa.

"Some of the Most Successful Businesses in the US Were Started By Entrepreneurs Over Age 50," *Business Insider.* November 12, 2014, by Sarah Schmalbruch.

"More Older Adults Are Becoming Inventors," *New York Times*. April 17, 2015, by Constance Gustke.

"Who Makes the Best Entrepreneurs? It's Not Who You Think: Why I'm Putting My Money on the Older Horse," March 30, 2015 by Michael Hyatt. Accessed from *michaelhyatt.com*.

## SECTION 3—Creating Your Legacy Map

"President George H.W. Bush Makes Parachute Jump for 90th Birthday," *People*. June 12, 2014, by Associated Press.

"Tips on Navigating the Midlife Stage," *USA Today*. April 25, 2011, by Kerry Hannon.

Marc Freedman. *Encore: Finding work that matters in the second half of life*. PublicAffairs, 2008.

James Clear. *Atomic Habits: An Easy and Proven Way to Build Good Habits*. Random House, 2018.

Rick Warren. *The Purpose Driven Life*. Zondervan, 2002.

"Olga Kotelko, a Canadian Track Star Well Into Her 90s Has Died," *The Globe and Mail*. June 25, 2014, by Tu Thanh Ha.

"Walt Disney Moves Up in Market Cap Rank." *Forbes Online*. Dividend Channel, contributor. (Appeared January 27, 2015 on *forbes.com*.)

Brian Tracy. *Goals! How to get everything you want – faster than you ever thought possible*. Berrett-Koehler Publishers, 2010.

'Building Your Company's Vision." *Harvard Business Review*, September-October 1996 Issue. By James C. Collins and Jerry I. Porras.

Jim Collins and Jerry Porras. *Built to Last: Successful Habits of Visionary Companies*. Harper Collins, 2004.

"How to Achieve Big, Hairy, Audacious Goals," *Inc.* magazine. November 1, 2012, by Leigh Buchanan.

"The Art of the Vision Board: How to Do It and Why a Bit of Woo is Good for the Soul." By Dr. Aviva Romm. December 7, 2014. Accessed online. (*avivaromm.com*)

"Dominican Research Cited in Forbes Article." By Dominican University of California. Undated web page. (*dominican.edu/dominicannews/dominican-research-cited-in-forbes-article.*)

Napoleon Hill. *Think and Grow Rich*. Ralston Publishing, 1953.

Ari Weinzweig. *A Lapsed Anarchist's Approach to Building a Great Business*. Zingerman's Press, 2010.

Check out Ari's other books, *Zingerman's Guide to Leadership (Parts 2 and 3)*, and *Zingerman's Business Secrets*. See more at *zingermans.com*.

John C. Maxwell. *The Five Levels of Leadership: Proven Steps to Maximize Your Potential*. Center Street, 2011.

*Infinitefamily.org* is a global mentoring organization dedicated to cultivating self-reliance in Africa's teens affected by HIV/AIDS and poverty.

Angela Duckworth. *Grit: The Power of Passion and Perseverance.* Simon & Schuster, 2016.

Verne Harnish. *Mastering the Rockefeller Habits: What You Must Do to Increase the Value of Your Growing Firm.* Gazelles Inc., 2002.

Chris McChesney, Sean Covey, Jim Huling. *The 4 Disciplines of Execution: Achieving Your Wildly Important Goals.* Free Press, 2010.

Peter H. Thomas. *Be Great: The Five Foundations of an Extraordinary Life In Business and Beyond.* Jon Wiley & Sons, Canada, 2009.

"Warren Buffet's 5-Step Process for Prioritizing True Success and Why Most People Never Do It," *Live Your Legend.* February 1, 2011 (*liveyourlegend.net*).

"World's Billionaires," *Forbes.* 2016 Ranking. Accessed at *forbes.com/ profile/warren-buffett/.*

Eric Barker. *Barking Up The Wrong Tree: The Surprising Science Behind Why Everything You Know About Success Is (Mostly) Wrong.* HarperOne, 2017.

Cal Newport. *Deep Work: Rules for Focused Success in a Distracted World.* Business Plus, 2012.

Greg McKeown. *Essentialism: The Disciplined Pursuit of Less*. Currency, 2014.

Akers, Paul A. *2 Second Lean Health: Aging in Reverse*. FastCap Press, 2015.

Akers, Paul A. *2 Second Lean: How to Grow People and Build a Lean Culture*. FastCap Press, 2012.

"Lean" resources and videos by Paul Akers at *2secondlean.com*.

Verne Harnish. *Scaling Up: How a Few Companies Make It and Why the Rest Don't*. Gazelles Inc., 2014.

"How Long Does It Take to Form a Habit?" *University College London*, August 4 2009. Quotes study by Phillippa Lally first published in *European Journal of Social Psychology* (*ucl.ac.uk/news-articles*).

Charles Duhigg. *The Power of Habit: Why We Do What We Do in Life and Business*. Random House, 2012.

Malcolm Gladwell. *Outliers: The Story of Success*. Little, Brown and Company, 2008.

Geoff Colvin. *Talent Is Overrated: What Really Separates World-Class Performers from Everybody Else*. Penguin Group, 2008.

Stephen R. Covey. *The 7 Habits of Highly Effective People*. Summit Books, 1989.

John C. Maxwell. *Failing Forward: Turning Mistakes into Stepping Stones.* Thomas Nelson, 2000.

## SECTION 4—You're Way Too Smart to Retire

"Many Americans Try Retirement, Then Change Their Minds," *New York Times.* March 30, 2018 by Paula Span.

Daniel DeNoon, reviewed by Louise Chang MD. "Early Retirement, Early Death?" *WebMD Health News.* October 20, 2005.

"Age at Retirement and Long-Term Survival of an Industrial Population." By US National Library of Medicine, National Institute of Health. October 29, 2005. (*ncbi.nlm.nih.gov/pmc/articles/PMC1273451.*)

"Retirement Will Kill You," *Bloomberg View.* June 11, 2013, by Peter Orszag (More articles at *bloombergview.com*).

Ad Vingerhoets and Maaike van Huijgevoort. "*Leisure sickness: An explorative study*" presented at American Psychosomatic Society on March 7, 2001.

"Out of the Ruins: Interview with Walker Percy," *Crisis Magazine.* July 1, 1989 by Scott Walter.

"Florida Syndrome," *Sun Sentinel.* March 20, 1989, by Diane Lade.

"Florida Syndrome Haunts Newcomers Looking for Eden," *LA Times.* April 16, 1989, by Brian Murphy of Associated Press.

"Judi Dench Interview: Retirement Is a Rude Word," *The Telegraph*. February 21, 2015, by John Hiscock.

"The History of Retirement, From Early Man to AARP," *New York Times*. March 21, 1999 by Mary-Lou Weisman.

"A Brief History of Retirement: It's a Modern Idea," *Seattle Times*. December 31, 2013, by Seattle Times Staff.

"How Retirement Was Invented," *The Atlantic*. October 24, 2014, by Sarah Laskow.

"Workplace Morale Heads Down: 70% of Americans Negative About Their Jobs, Gallup Study Shows," *New York Daily News*. June 24, 2013, by Beth Stebner.

Earl Nightingale. *Lead the Field*. Audio Books by Nightingale-Conant, 1987 (*nightingale.com*).

"Maslow's Hierarchy of Needs," *Simply Psychology*. McLeod, S. A. 2014. Accessed from *simplypsychology.org/maslow.html*.

Chip Conley. *Peak: How Great Companies Get Their Mojo From Maslow*. Jossey-Bass, 2007.

See Chip Conley's TED Talk and sign up for his newsletter at *chipconley.com*. He's all about "creating transformation at the intersection of business and psychology."

Peter H. Thomas. *Be Great: The Five Foundations of an Extraordinary Life In Business and Beyond*. Jon Wiley & Sons, Canada, 2009.

"Work in Retirement: Myths and Motivations." A *Merrill Lynch Retirement Study* conducted in partnership with Age Wave in 2014. Accessed from *agewave.com/research/Home-in-Retirement-Report.pdf.*

"10,000 Boomers Turn 65 Every Day. Can Medicare and Social Security Handle It?" By Eric Pianin. May 9, 2017. The Fiscal Times (*thefiscaltimes.com/2017/05/09*).

"Baby Boomers Retire" By Russell Heimlich. December 29, 2010. Pew Research (*pewresearch.org/fact-tank/2010/12/29/baby/boomers/retire*).

"A Billion Shades of Grey." *The Economist.* April 26, 2014.

"More Older Workers Making Up Labor Force," *Los Angeles Times.* September 4, 2012, by Don Lee.

Peter Diamandis and Steven Kotler. *Abundance: The Future Is Better Than You Think.* Free Press, a division of Simon & Schuster, 2012.

Chris Farrell. *Unretirement: How Baby Boomers Are Changing the Way We Think About Work, Community, and the Good Life.* Bloomsbury Press, 2014.

"Many Baby Boomers Reluctant to Retire," *Gallup Economy Series.* January 20, 2014, by Jim Harter and Sangeeta Abrawal (*gallup.com/poll/166952/baby-boomers-reluctant-retire.aspx*).

Douglas Rushkoff. *Present Shock: When Everything Happens Now.* Current, 2013.

"I Deserve It: As the 18-30 Generation Matures, An Ethicist Says Those Wanting a Kinder, Gentler America May Be Disappointed," *Philadelphia Inquirer.* December 21, 1990, by David O'Reilly. (Follow Michael Josephson at *whatwillmatter.com.*)

"Why Baby Boomers Are Ditching Retirement To Launch Their Own Businesses." Forbes. January 5, 2018, by Brian Scudamore.

## SECTION 5—Three Drivers to Second-Half Success

John O'Leary. *On Fire: The 7 Choices to Ignite a Radically Inspired Life.* Gallery Books, 2016.

Charles Handy. *The Age of Unreason.* Harvard Business School Press, 1989.

"I Embraced Henry James' Fight Against Complacency," *The UK Guardian.* August 28, 2015, by Colin Toibin.

View the 2014 movie "Mr. Turner" starring Timothy Spall as eccentric English painter J.M.W. Turner. Nominated for four Academy Awards, the film explores the last quarter century of this late-blooming genius.

"A Conversation with Frank McCourt," *Hartford Courant.* August 29, 1999, by Owen McNally.

Frank McCourt. *Teacher Man*. Scribner, 2005.

Jung quotes drawn from historical data and numerous accounts. References include: "The Jung Page" for educational resources (*cgjungpage.org*). Also see "Jung Society of Washington" (*jung.org*) and "Carl Jung Resources" (*carl-jung.net*).

Bob Buford. *Half Time: Changing Your Game Plan from Success to Significance*. Zondervan, 2015.

Leo Tolstoy. *The Death of Ivan Ilyich*. White Crow Books, 2010.

## SECTION 6—Staying Ahead of the Game

Salim Ismail with Michael S. Malone and Yuri Van Geest. *Exponential Organizations: Why New Organizations Are Ten Times Better, Faster, and Cheaper Than Yours*. Diversion Books, 2014.

"100 Years Old and Water Skiing," *ABC News*. November 20, 2005, by Desiree Abid.

"Why Bodybuilding at 93 is a Good Idea," TED Talk featuring Dr. Charles Eugster. Also referenced was Dr. Eugster's website *charleseugster.net*.

Peter Diamandis and Steven Kotler. *Abundance: The Future Is Better Than You Think*. Free Press, a division of Simon & Schuster, 2012.

Anna Quindlen. *A Short Guide to a Happy Life*. Random House, 2000.

Angela Duckworth. *Grit: The Power of Passion and Perseverance.* Simon & Schuster, 2016.

Alvise Cornaro. *Writings on the Sober Life: The Art and Grace of Living Long.* Translated by Hiroko Fudemoto. University of Toronto Press, 2014.

"10,000 Boomers Turn 65 Every Day. Can Medicare and Social Security Handle It?" *The Fiscal Times.* May 9, 2017, by Eric Pianin *(thefiscaltimes.com/2017/05/09).*

"Baby Boomers Retire" By Russell Heimlich. December 29, 2010. Pew Research *(pewresearch.org/fact-tank/2010/12/29/baby/ boomers/retire).*

David Snowdon. *Aging with Grace: What the Nun Study Can Teach Us About Leading longer, Healthier, and More Meaningful Lives.* Bantam Books, 2001.

John Wooden and Jay Carty. *Coach Wooden's Pyramid of Success Playbook.* Revell, 2005.

Andrew J. Sherman. *Harvesting Intangible Assets: Uncover Hidden Revenue in Your Company's Intellectual Property.* Amacom, 2011.

Information on Joy Mangano from *joymangano.com* and *wikipedia. com.*

Bruce Grierson. *What Makes Olga Run?* Henri Holt, 2014. More excellent resources at *brucegrierson.com.*

"Super Senior Study Looking for Volunteers," *Vancouver Courier*. June 5, 2015, by Sandra Thomas (citing research by Dr. Angela Brooks-Wilson).

"A Theory of Human Motivation." An internet resource from *Classics in the History of Psychology*. (Christopher Green, York University). Originally published in *Psychological Review* by A.H. Maslwow, 1943.

Bruce Grierson. *What Makes Olga Run?* Henri Holt, 2014. More excellent resources at *brucegrierson.com*.

"Olga Kotelko, a Canadian Track Star Well Into Her 90s Has Died," *The Globe and Mail*. June 25, 2014, by Tu Thanh Ha.

"How Driving a Taxi Changes London Cabbie's Brains," *Wired UK*. September 9, 2011, by Mark Brown. (Quoting sources including *Current Biology*.)

Maguire, Woollett, and Spiers. "London taxi drivers and bus drivers: a structural MRI and neuropsychological analysis." *Hippocampus*, 2006; 16(12):1091-101.

Jim Rohn. *Leading an Inspired Life*. Nightingale-Conant, 1996.

"Why Leaders Must be Readers," *Forbes*. August 3, 2012, by Kelsey Meyer.

"100 Years Old. 5 World Records," *New York Times*. September 21, 2015, by Karen Crouse.

'100-Year-Old Santa Clara Track Star Keeps Breaking Records," *San Francisco CBS*. September 23, 2015, by John Ramos.

"The ageing body," *The Guardian*. April 22, 2004 by Germaine Greer.

Chris Crowley and Henry Lodge. *Younger Next Year: A Guide to Living Like 50 Until You're 80 or Beyond*. Workman Publishing Company, 2005.

"The New Age of Much Older Age," *Time*. February 23, 2015, by Laura L. Carstensen (pages. 69-70).

# SECTION 7—It All Comes Down to Character

Stephen R. Covey. *The 7 Habits of Highly Effective People*. Summit Books, 1989.

Stephen R. Covey. *Principle-Centered Leadership*. Summit Books, 1991.

Jim Collins and Jerry Porras. *Built to Last: Successful Habits of Visionary Companies*. Harper Collins, 2004.

"One Role Model to Another," *Sports Illustrated*. June 14, 1993, by Karl Malone.

Rick Warren. *The Purpose Driven Life*. Zondervan, 2002.

Os Guinness. *Character Counts*. The Trinity Forum & Baker Books, 1999.

"Are Workplace Distractions Costing You Time and Money?" *All Business*. Undated online article by Susan Wilson Solovic (*allbusiness.com*).

Stephen R. Covey and Roger Merrill, *First Things First*. Free Press, a division of Simon & Schuster, 1996.

David Brooks. *The Road to Character*. Random House, 2015. (View Brooks's Ted Talk at *roadtocharacter.com*. Read Brooks's *New York Times* columns at *nytimes.com/column/david-brooks*.)

Greg McKeown. Essentialism: The Disciplined Pursuit of Less. Currency, 2014.

Made in the USA
Middletown, DE
16 October 2023

40883874R00177